HOW WILL YOU BUILD AND SELL YOUR BUSINESS

"This book is packed full of useful information and ideas which will be immediately useful to anyone starting or running a small business."

– Karl Ward

HOW WILL YOU BUILD AND SELL YOUR BUSINESS

AND MAKE LOADS OF CASH IN THE PROCESS

CHRIS HAMBLY

Published in Falmouth, UK, by Audana Ltd.
ISBN-10: 1521769427
ISBN-13: 978-1521769423
Printed by Audana Ltd
Audana, PO Box 331, Falmouth, TR11 9DL, UK

DEDICATION

To my dad for giving me the fighting skills to always push forward.

To my mum for giving me the self-belief and to chase my dreams.

To my wife, Jo, for putting up with my continual restlessness and desire to move.

Disclaimer

This book and the content provided herein are simply for educational purposes, and do not take the place of legal advice from your solicitor or attorney. Every effort has been made to ensure that the content provided in this book is accurate and helpful for you at publishing time. However, this is not an exhaustive treatment of the subjects. No liability is assumed for losses or damages due to the information provided. You are responsible for your own choices, actions, and results.

Having said that if you are looking for someone that can tell you how to focus and what has worked for business growth and sale, read on.

TABLE OF CONTENTS

Preface

I've just sold my second business and made a 2000% return on my investment in 5 years. I'm delighted.

When I first thought about writing this book I was full of enthusiasm and couldn't wait to begin. Like other projects that I find myself becoming interested in I'm eager to throw myself at them and give them my all, this was no different; or so I thought.

Yet when it was time to start I was left looking at a blank white screen in Google Docs, and suddenly horrified that I had no clue about how to begin a book.

The book concept was actually something that was a second thought. The first thought I had was that now that I had sold my second business I felt I had some good things to tell. Things that would make a difference to other people that own a small business and want to grow it.

So being of an entrepreneurial mind, and someone that enjoys teaching, I figured out I would write an online course, a multi-part course about how I built this particular tourism-based business into a turn-key solution, making it attractive to a buyer, and eventual sale.

The trouble I had with the course concept was that this business was more than just a business to me. I had significant personal interest in it, so many stories to tell, stories that wouldn't come across in a course or a manual. This led me to believe that indeed, a book would be a good approach because it would allow me to just talk to you, express my feelings, share my pain and hopefully get across what it is I have to give you in a far more compelling way.

I've actually done both, and the Academy course can be found here: chrishambly.com where you can sign up for the full blown tuition.

I've realised that over the years I have written a lot of information about businesses and a fair amount of that I have republished on my website. It makes sense to consolidate a lot of information for your easy perusal.

Lastly I just want to say I'm just like you, I'm no different than the next guy. I do not have special powers or magic tricks. However if I notice one thing about myself that I do not see in many others around me it is this: I graft harder, work longer hours, go deeper, push more, ask questions, fear little. Success is just hard work, with the ability to embrace failure and learn, it's not good luck. Well perhaps it is maybe just a little luck too.

So, here is my book, I do hope it helps you in your own endeavours.

Once upon a time…

(Every business has a story)

Falmouth is a small town of about 28,000 residents, steeped in maritime trade, in the county of Cornwall, England, which is about 5 hours by car south west of London. Being a significant port Falmouth is famed for manufacturing superyachts for the rich and famous as well as conducting refits for naval vessels and huge ocean-going cargo vessels.

Over the last 60 years Falmouth's main industry has become tourism. With beautiful golden sandy beaches and a huge growth in marinas, bars, restaurants it's become a favoured seaside holiday destination.

As a boy I have very vivid memories of spending time with my father on Custom House Quay, Falmouth. Dad was a marine engineer by trade and at some point he decided to take a leap of faith and buy a pleasure boat.

Dad's boat, "*Heather*", was a splendid wooden passenger boat that he sweated blood and tears over in getting her up to an immaculate state, fit for passengers to enjoy river trips. *Heather* worked out of Custom House Quay along with various other passenger boats.

I'm talking about the 1970s here, the heyday when tourists would flood to the seaside for their holidays, way before cheap budget airlines and package holidays to the Mediterranean become the norm. Falmouth would bc buzzing and the population during the summer months would swell enormously.

The entrance to the quay is where all the boat operators would be touting their wares, handing out leaflets. This was a lively and colourful place to be hanging out as a boy. Looking back now this gave me a strong impression of what it was to be pushy for business. These men were hungry, their livelihoods literally depended on it. No customers resulted in no earnings, which of course meant no bacon to take home for the family. There was a lot of fiercely competitive one-upmanship. Each season on the quay would last only from Easter through to about October half-term, these operators had to mostly earn their annual takings during that period.

As well as the pleasure cruises, river trips, shark fishing and passenger ferries, Custom House Quay basin (a Dutch designed quay with a large square tidal area inside) also had a thriving self-drive boat business operating over 30 cabin boats available for tourists to drive themselves. The sight was spectacular, over 30 self-operated cabin boats coming and going all day long every day. There were two main fleets, 15 boats belonging to "Moonfleet" owned at the time by Derek and 15 boats belonging to "Sunfleet" owned at the time by Tony and Arnold. As a young teenage boy I would look on in envy at the lads who would be doing the grunt work of washing them down, fuelling them up, driving them to and fro the steps for the customers to get on. Chas Cox was one such lad. You'll hear a lot about Chas through this book.

At the start of one season which I think must have been around 1982/83 Dad spoke to me after a conversation with Derek who ran the Moonfleet boats. *"You start tomorrow mate"*, Dad said. This was the beginning of my love affair with the Quay, I was now a "Quay Boy".

I would finish school and then make my way down to the quay to work on the boats, and then each weekend I would spend both Saturday and Sunday working and during the school holidays I'd be on the Quay every day. It was hard work, but to be honest it never felt like hard work, even to this day. You can just imagine a young teenage boy playing boats all day long, surrounded by fresh tourists every day, the beautiful girls in their summer clothes, the underage drinking, the odd cheeky cigarette, the look of envy of every other teenage boy, the dashing away in the speedboat to go water skiing after work, picking up a Chinese for tea, or a bag of chips on the boss, it was quite literally the best job I've have ever had.

WHERE WAS I?

(It's important to know where you're from)

Fast forward about 25 years.

I had graduated with a Masters in Open and Distance Education and become a seasoned digital guru having built and sold an online school in the field of music technology (first of its kind in the world). I was generating a five figure monthly income through consultancy contracts providing services such eLearning, websites, SEO, social media, email marketing and strategic consultation. I had worked on projects for big brands like Coca-Cola, BP, Capital One, Direct Line. I was based in London and very much part of the digerati.

Jo and myself had two children (now we have three), with our youngest just over a year old when we moved back to Cornwall. We'd just secured a massive mortgage on our new dream house and things were fabulous.

Then devastating news came to the front door.

I had made the oldest mistake in the book. 80% of my income was coming from 20% of my clients. The "big" client's business got acquired and my services would no longer be needed for the following year. I was brought to my knees in an instant. The crushing pain I felt, the intense financial pressure that would soon be looming was almost too much to bear.

I would not wish a shock like that on anyone. What could I do? We had moved back from London because we wanted the dream life back in our home town, with the spoils of handsome income generated from the city. Would I have to move back, work during the weeks in London and come home for the weekends? The thought of that was too painful, I'd not see my kids grow up. I felt somewhat powerless and weak.

It was during this period of self-questioning, with I must say amazing support from my wife (I really can't sing her praises enough here), that I dusted myself off and started looking around me with my eyes wide open. I needed to do something to gather my thoughts, buy me some time and consider my next move.

THERE IS ALWAYS AN AVENUE

I called Chas Cox, you know, the lad from the boats back in the 80s!

Chas had always missed the boats and when he had an opportunity to buy the boat business he did. He bought the Moonfleet and Sunfleet boats some 13 years or so before this period and ran it as more of a hobby.

After so many years of not talking to Chas apart from the odd catch up over a quick beer I unloaded my situation. His warm response was as if nothing had changed, "I need someone to run the boats this year, Chris".

It was a win for the both of us, his boat business partner Tony was getting on a bit and didn't want to do it anymore, I needed time, head space and some form of income. We struck up a deal, where I got paid a flat rate and then a bonus on anything over a certain amount per day.

I started a few days later.

From wearing a handmade suit from Savile Row and visiting clients in swanky board rooms with 60 foot glass tables and waterfalls, I was now back on the Quay wearing cut off ripped jeans, a t-shirt covered in salt, oil and sweat every day, and I loved every minute of it.

I was hungry too, my mind was focussed, I was searching for a way out, determined and fighting hard every day. The manual labour of running the boats 6 days a week was good for me, I felt in shape, I was sun kissed and breathing in amazing salty air. Meeting tourists every day and interacting got me out of my slump pretty quickly.

This first season of me back on the boats saw me take the train up to London a few times, with the notion of working back there for a PR or digital agency. I would put the suit on and shake hands with the managing directors with my now rough workman hands and sun tanned face. It was a strange sensation. Something about it didn't feel right, almost false, and I started focussing more close to home and starting picking up local clients that wanted digital solutions. I soon picked up some good traction and over the following years got back up to earning 5 figures monthly again, mostly from local contracts.

I do believe it was the head space of the first year back on the Quay that helped me get back on my feet.

What do you want your business to be?

(Building solid foundations has to be your start point)

How often have you found yourself working "in" the business with no time for working "on" the business? Have you found yourself doing everything and feeling like you are getting nowhere? When was the last time you reviewed each and every aspect of your business? This section focuses on how to build the foundations of your business to be solid and process oriented.

STATE OF THE BUSINESS

At this time the business was still called Moonfleet and Sunfleet. Chas had just a handful of boats ready to let, both red painted boats and blue painted boats, a few months later we had four (with one more in a field collecting leaves). Chas was a busy man and it was he who had to do all the boat maintenance, get them ready for launch etc., a big ask. I just turned up and ran the day to day operation and sold the hires.

The state of the website was atrocious. It was I think just 3 pages, maybe 4 and a few pictures, something that had been put together and forgotten about. I have a larger section further into the book which talks about the importance of a website so I'll leave this short here for now. The pricing was wrong, the marketing was almost non-existent.

At this point Chas was not investing a great deal of time more than necessary into the business, he'd had it for about 15 years at this point and was probably somewhat jaded by it. I think he loved being outside when the boats were running mind you, but his business partner had pretty much already retired so no doubt it would have been a hassle to run it, being so busy himself with other commitments.

The mechanics of the business were identical to how they always were. That is, put a sign up saying "boats for hire", and wait for people to walk buy and take an interest. The footfall though on the quay was not what it had been 25 years previously, which considering this was the main sales channel for the business, wasn't great! Additional sales channels were needed.

TIP: Evaluate your business honestly, is it really what you think it could be?

KNOW YOUR STRENGTHS

Chas is a fantastic technical man, he just loved to tinker and keep the boats running mechanically. By his own admission he is not a marketing man or someone that works "on" the business necessarily but "in" the business. That's his strength, and he's damn good at it too. You understand what I mean by working "in" the business as opposed to "on" it?

What my experience brought to the party was an entrepreneurial streak and the ability to take a step back and look at how we could change things and improve areas for the better of us both. Basically put, how to generate more cash. This is considered working "on" the business. What can we do to change things for the better? What can I do that will create more profit? What can we do that will grow the turn-over? Working "in" the business continually means you can never step back and grow things further, or make progress as you're forever busy just running the show. If this is you, beware because your business can stagnate from lack of growth, diversity and strategic thinking.

After a great first season Chas wanted me as his partner in the business, replacing Tony. Chas is not a naive man, he knew I could grow things and improve the business, together we'd be a formidable force. Tony wanted a very small dollop of cash, not even half the actual price of the boats, and there were only five at the time; it was well under-priced. So I bought in and the business was now half mine. I actually had very little money at the time; I was really strapped for cash, but I knew I'd reap rewards further down the road, easily. Both Chas and I knew our end game would be to grow and sell the business, effectively turning it into a turn-key solution.

When I talk about turn-key I do literally mean to bring the business up to such a state that someone off the street could be handed the keys and be up and running trading. The business should not in any form be dependent on an individual person within it. The job roles and skill sets should be known and replaceable.

Now, let's get into the nuts and bolts of what I did, the bit you really want to read.

TIP: Identify your key strengths. What feels easy, a breeze, what comes natural to you? Try to align your role with that. Let others do the things you cannot do, or do not enjoy.

RELATIONSHIPS

There are of course two main areas for consideration when discussing relationships.

1. Business relationships
2. Family relationships

Let's look at each in turn.

BUSINESS RELATIONSHIPS

Coming on board with this business meant I had to initially tread pretty carefully with Chas. Having garnered some hefty experience in the city with large brands along with growing and selling former businesses, I had so many ideas on how to improve this small business. I can only imagine what Chas must have thought. I know I can storm right in and be somewhat overbearing sometimes. I was aware of this and tried to be patient and choose my timing to get Chas on board and understand my thinking.

If you have a partner in your business you will understand my sentiments here. It really is so very important to manage these relationships with care and attention. You must always remember it is just business, and that is hard when you have such personal attachment to it, but it is just business and worth reminding yourself of that, regularly.

I was fortunate that Chas is such a calm and reflective guy, we were a good team with very different skills, and we managed each other very well. None of what you are about to read would be possible unless we had this fundamental mutual respect for each other.

If you are thinking of a business partner, choose wisely, it's the glue in everything. I would not consider going into business with many people, but with Chas, it was a very easy decision to make. You should make this your number one priority to consider before you do anything, if you have a business partner, or are thinking about one.

FAMILY RELATIONSHIPS

Needless to say family relationships are vital part in the jigsaw of your business. These relationships can be with your spouse, siblings, kids, parents. Anyone that is closely involved in your personal life becomes fully affected by your business.

Running a small business, or any business for that matter, means the buck really does stop with you. You are not in a situation of being able to walk away. You are the one that is having to deal with resolving issues at 4am. You are the one that has to ensure things get fixed. You are the one that will be at the family dinner table for a celebratory meal, receive a phone call and have to leave.

Owning a business is not for the faint hearted. If you like going to work at 9am, and then going home and forgetting about it at 5pm, then having your own business is not for you. Stop reading this book now and give it to someone else.

Your business is not "work", it's not a "job".

Your business is a lifestyle choice with you as the leader. The business is actually another one of your family members. This way of thinking about your business needs to be conveyed and understood by your close family members, as they will soon been affected by it. When there is understanding, there will less likely be conflict.

Of course running and (hopefully) growing your own business means you have amazing flexibility in your life and hopefully earn a lot more money than the 9-5 in a much shorter space of time.

STRATEGIC OBJECTIVE

You've heard previously that I had a business prior to Falmouth Boat Hire, in fact a couple or so. You can say I'm entrepreneurial. I've studied, researched, talked about, read and consumed a heap of information about entrepreneurship. Some of it has been dull and some of it absolutely fantastic. One such fantastic book is called The e-Myth by Michael Gerber (highly recommend you read that). Michael talks about setting out a strategic objective as soon as possible.

A strategic objective is important for lots of reasons, but what the hell is it?

A strategic objective is a top level list of objectives that will guide your business on the right path, it is your map, your journey. It becomes your bible, your operating guide of sorts.

When I first spoke about this with Chas he thought I had gone completely nuts and lost my mind. I think he even said "are you serious?" I chuckle now, yes I was serious.

If you want to take something somewhere you need a plan, you need to know where you are going, or more to the point how you are going to get there. If you just do the same thing every day without a plan of what you are trying to achieve and how, you will forever be doing the same thing every day and going nowhere.

So your Strategic Objective then should be a list of who you are and what you do.

Let's get down to business.

OUR STRATEGIC OBJECTIVE

This is what I drew up, the one that Chas couldn't believe I had written.

1. We are the highest-quality boat hire service in Cornwall.
2. Our fundamental strategy is to relentlessly "work" the systems of the business to perfect our operating procedures.
3. Falmouth Boat Hire's primary offering is 12 hour, 7 day a week boat hire between Easter and October half-term.
4. Our guiding document is this, the Strategic Objective.
5. Through intense commitment to our employees and procedures, we will contribute to the success of satisfied customers.
6. Our business is complex, with many human, mechanical, and computer systems in simultaneous motion. Success depends on refined communication and organisational processes, dedicated staff, documented point-of-sale procedures, first class boats and equipment, rigorous quality assurance with continuous measurement, assertive innovation, intense planned maintenance/system improvement, aggressive and measured marketing, and relentless attention to detail in every nook and cranny.
7. Competitive advantages include thoughtful customer service that is immediate and consistent, latest online marketing techniques, no experience necessary products, safe for families, strong central location.
8. We constantly refine and improve all internal systems and mechanisms.

9. To grow, we proceed with an "if we build it, they will come" philosophy, juxtaposed with assertive marketing efforts.

10. Although we tightly direct Falmouth Boat Hire's operation through guiding documentation, we will modify that documentation immediately if an enhancement can be made: "Our operational framework is rigid, but that framework can be modified instantly".

11. We segment responsibilities into specialised "expert compartments" with appropriate cross-training among departments. We have backup personnel for all positions.

12. Primary vertical markets include tourism and local residents and students.

This was not just a list designed to inflate our egos. In fact at the time it was written we were not the highest quality boat hire company in Cornwall, the boats were a bit tired, the customer service was OK, the branding was crap, we didn't have aggressive marketing in place. BUT we had to begin thinking we were the best, we had to strive to be so, and we did in fact become so.

I printed this strategic objective document, laminated it, and stuck it up in our van (our office at the time). I also ensured all the lads that worked with us read it, and kept referring them to it.

Do not underestimate the significance of this document. Chas by his own admission eventually said "oh yes it works", which he explained to our eventual buyer when we were through the point of sale.

IT'S A TEAM MENTALITY

For this to work it is absolutely critical that you get all of your staff on the same page.

In our case for example all staff needed to be on board with "Through intense commitment to our employees and procedures, we will contribute to the success of satisfied customers." They all had to be aligned with "Our fundamental strategy is to relentlessly "work" the systems of the business to perfect our operating procedures."

You have to get everyone on board with your strategic objectives, even the objectives that individual staff do not actually carry out personally. It's almost like the ten commandments of your business.

With these strategic objectives in place, your business will now have a mission - but be prepared to implement change especially when things do not work, you must be flexible. If one of your team finds a better way of doing something, perhaps with more efficacy or with greater impact on customer service, be smart enough to immediately implement the idea. You should let your team know they can suggest ideas, encourage them to perfect the business with you. Even if you disagree with the idea suggested, you are at least offering your staff the opportunity to be interested in positive thoughts for improvement. Most people like to be heard and appreciated, made to feel important.

So your strategic objective is definitely not a business plan in the traditional sense, not like those ones that are obsolete as soon as they are written. A strategic objective is more a guiding document of principles, or ways of being and thinking about your business for you and your team.

I've never written a traditional business plan, I don't consider one to be of much value, they are just ways of getting cash from bankers, and always too rigid to be of any use.

TIP: Take some time to write your strategic objective, use mine as a start point. The task of writing things down, and telling others is a commitment in itself. Think it, believe it, and make it happen. BUT document it first.

INCORPORATE THE BUSINESS

One of the first things we did was change the name from Moonfleet Sunfleet to Falmouth Boat Hire and incorporate it as a limited company. I mean Moonfleet/Sunfleet, seriously? I know this name was ages old and had always been so but, no, no, no, it had to go.

Never hang onto things just because they have always been that way, it will cease your creativity. You must be willing to flip things completely on their head. Too much nostalgia will shroud your business in a fog, and you'll never see through it.

Incorporating the business as a limited company meant that Falmouth Boat Hire was a legal entity in its own right with Chas and myself as directors of it. This made sense on lots of levels not least that if anything bad legally or financially were to raise its head it would be the company that would be responsible not us personally.

This separation of you and the business as the legal entity is very important if you have debts. If for example you are incorporated, your house would never be in jeopardy. Being a sole trader is all well and good, with less documentation necessary and legal requirements but it can be a horrific experience if things ever do go wrong. My advice is don't take that chance. Luckily this has not happened to me, but I wouldn't risk it either.

Incorporating the business also gave the business some kudos, some weight, some seriousness. If you are a small business it's definitely worth a consideration going down this route.

Financially speaking and simply put an incorporated company pays you a salary, often a low one for tax reasons, and then the company pays out dividends to you when it makes a profit.

Legally speaking, if something terrible happens the business is responsible not the individuals.

TIP: Seek advice from your accountant here about which is best for your situation.

ACCOUNTANCY

In running businesses I have found that the accountancy requirements are best left to the professionals. I'm definitely not an accountant, I have almost zero interest in bean counting and I'm useless at accountancy for that reason. OK sure I can compute math, but it just bores me.

As well as being incredibly bored from looking at spreadsheets and profit/loss figures I also feel that if you have resources around you that excel in areas that you do not, let those resources do this work for you. Your time is best spent on the areas of your business that will help it grow. If you could calculate your hourly rate, what it costs the business for one hour of your time, it would be high, this should not be wasted on accountancy. When you get too involved with accountancy you are working "in" the business, not "on" it. A business owner needs to be working "on" the business as much as possible.

From your accountant you want top level figures. You should be interested in how much the business has earnt, and how much it has spent in being able to earn that figure. You should also be interested in knowing what your main costs are. What are the big overheads and why are they so high? What can you change or perfect more in your business that will reduce the overheads, therefore increase profit.

Quite often you can find ways of reducing overheads. Sometimes you can just run up higher than necessary overheads unwittingly and before you know it a chunk of cash is disappearing.

So definitely look at your overheads, it makes more sense to increase your profit by cutting costs, than spending additional funds on advertising to obtain new customers.

Accountants also bring other really interesting angles to your books on where to spend, where to save and generally how you can achieve the maximum tax benefits.

TIP: Look for an accountancy firm that will offer you a fixed price monthly subscription that will cover your annual company returns and also periodic advice when you need it.

TERMS AND CONDITIONS

Not long after incorporating the business to Falmouth Boat Hire it became apparent we should also give the business a degree of formality with hire agreements. So I hunted around the Internet looking for standard hire agreement contracts and cobbled together a set of our own, applicable to our unique business.

The agreement was then printed onto duplicate carbon copy forms that a customer would have to sign before leaving the Quay. It gave us a safe position to negotiate from in case of damages or anything else untoward. It also gave the customer the same assurance. They knew what was permitted and what was not.

Reading the Terms and Conditions was also a process requirement that had to be completed before a customer could make a payment online. These Terms and Conditions were also given a lot of visibility on our website. Of course before these T&Cs existed the "rules" were always pretty grey and would be whatever we just said on the day, which of course is not good.

Here they are.

1. Cancellations due to weather conditions (if the weather is deemed unsuitable to let) are made at the absolute discretion of Falmouth Boat Hire.
2. Falmouth Boat Hire has the right to turn away any person(s) deemed not suitable to hire.
3. If Falmouth Boat Hire cancels your booking you will first be offered a choice of an alternative date or entitled to a full refund if the dates are not suitable for you.
4. Should you cancel your trip with less than 24 hours' notice you will not be entitled to a refund, nor will you be entitled

to a refund if you decide the weather conditions are not suitable for you. For example rain or cloudy conditions do not constitute a valid reason for a cancellation. If Falmouth Boat Hire is operating then all bookings are to be honoured.

5. If the weather is deemed too dangerous to explore the River Fal estuary we may still operate within the inner harbour which is more sheltered. You will be entitled to change the date of your trip though you will not be offered a refund.

6. For all bookings there must be someone of at least 21 years of age responsible for the party.

7. Boats are not permitted to carry more than 6 lives. This includes new born babies and toddlers, 6 lives is 6 lives.

8. If you or any of your party has any medical condition (e.g. diabetes, epilepsy etc.), it is advised that you tell us on arrival, should you become ill, we will then be able to get the best medical attention for you.

9. Falmouth Boat Hire is not responsible for any injury that you may suffer whatsoever whilst embarking or disembarking from any of our boats or whilst on any of our boats. If you become injured you agree to not hold Falmouth Boat Hire accountable.

10. Please feel free to bring cameras, video cameras or binoculars. Many people have brought them and taken fantastic pictures, but please be aware that Falmouth Boat Hire can take no responsibility for your property, should it get wet or damaged, this goes for clothes or any other property, whilst on-board and also left behind.

11. No alcohol is allowed on board and if you or any of your party are deemed unfit to hire a boat through alcohol then you will be refused entry onto our boats and you will not receive a refund.

12. If you choose to return your boat earlier than booked you will not be entitled to any refund. If you are reported as being a disturbance on the water or behaving inappropriately we reserve the right to ask you to return to port and you will not be eligible for a refund.

These Terms and Conditions proved very useful to the business and helped our team out in quite a few situations. The weather points were often relaxed a little. For example, if it rains it is still absolutely safe to rent a boat, the customer just gets wet but the business can still trade as normal. However, being so customer service centred we decided to relax on this rule and call customers giving them the option of cancellation should they wish.

For us it was far better to have a customer sing our praises regarding attention to their experience than to force them to go out in the pouring rain and have a shitty day. This paid off on many occasions and we even had a customer write on TripAdvisor how great that was, even though they had not even set foot on a boat!

Do put your customers first, do it.

In summary this section considered the importance of building solid foundations by being brutally honest in analysing the state of your business, understanding your own strengths, weaknesses and relationships. Recall that the Strategic Objective is a highly important document that sets the scene, the road map for your business. It is a set of top level statements that cover all areas of your business. From these top level statements you can derive business processes for each area. A process for accounting, marketing, operation etc.

Begin today, right now by sketching out your first draft of your   Strategic   Objective.

How do you want your business to look?

(Your parents were right - first impressions really do count)

How many times have you been put off by a grubby-looking shop front? Do you remember bad customer service you've had? How many times have you used a business based on recommendations? This section focuses on how to build your brand based on your objectives and values, who you want to attract, and why it's important to maintain a consistent marketing message.

BRANDING, WHAT IS IT?

Branding identifies your business, be it a name, symbol or tone of voice. Branding is a differentiation point for your business from your competitors.

When you create your brand it is important to be consistent with it through all your communication touch points, and over time. It's a statement of your company, what your company represents and how you wish your business to be perceived.

However, a brand is not just a logo and a colour scheme, it is an emotional impact with a customer. It is the feeling you get when you walk into McDonalds anywhere in the world. It is the entire experience a customer engages with. The fact of the matter is you have to earn branding, it is a customer's experience. Creating a fancy logo and luscious colour scheme will not work alone. If the experience does not live up to the customer's expectation time and time again it doesn't matter how much you spend on branding, it will fail.

WHAT IS YOUR BUSINESS?

You need to think about what your business represents and what do your services represent for a customer.

Start thinking about adjectives. Is your business dangerous, safe, loyal, challenging, cheap, expensive, exclusive, empowering, fun or serious?

Your business cannot be all things to all people, you must decide what your ideal customer is and work from there.

Don't ever try to accommodate everyone, it's a slippery road to a failing business, you can help yourself choose your ideal customer with good branding.

WHAT IS FALMOUTH BOAT HIRE?

When I started to consider what Falmouth Boat Hire was I quickly realised I wanted to attract the following "ideal" customer:

<u>Families with disposable income.</u>

I wanted to <u>not</u> attract single men, youths, stag parties, or people looking for a quick bargain. These would not be appropriate for a boat rental business. For a start single men in rental boats, stag parties? What a recipe for disaster that would be! People looking for a bargain? No thank you!

When I initially took on the business it was attracting all of these types of people, which was not suited for this business in any shape or form. It had to change.

Therefore I went about purposefully designing the branding to attract families with disposable income that are generally, level-headed, cautious, caring, safety conscious, risk averse and looking to spend good money on a quality family experience.

IT'S IMPORTANT TO COMMUNICATE YOUR BRAND CONSISTENTLY

It's very important to be consistent when it comes to communicating your brand.

Think about some major brand like Coke vs a generic brand. Coke has an impressive worldwide brand strategy that is consistent and never failing, same for McDonald's.

When you visit the local McDonalds, you expect a consistent experience time and time again. In fact anywhere in the world you expect this, and you'll get it time and time again. I've been in McDonald's in United Kingdom, Denmark, USA, Dubai, and countless other countries and the experience is always identical, consistent and the food tastes the same every single time.

This is very much part of consistent branding, but it's not just branding of course. Conceptually consistency runs right through their whole strategic objective, worldwide.

I wanted Falmouth Boat Hire to be consistent in every single aspect. This then needed a communication process, a process for how branding is conveyed. Have you considered how your brand is communicating?

VALUE AND PERCEPTION

You need to dig into the emotional aspect of branding and how to match that relatedness with your ideal customer.

Value is often not just what someone receives in their hands, in fact it is often not.

People want an experience, purchases are as much about lifestyle choices as anything else, particularly in the tourism sector.

Sure, we can be attracted to how many, how much, what do I get, yet Costa Coffee shops are always full, and they sell expensive coffee. We visit Costa because we identify and associate ourselves with the brand and lifestyle, the feel. There is immense value there, it is intangible.

Being able to create this value is golden, and should form part of your plan.

BASIC QUESTIONS TO ASK YOURSELF

What is the mission of your business? - This should come from your strategic objective that I covered previously.

What benefits do your business and products provide to me? - Think not in terms of how great your product is, think in terms of what benefits it gives me. Nobody really cares about how good you say you are, they only care about the benefits for them. Do not let your ego get in the way of this important fact. You'll see this played out so often on company websites. Company text will state ineffective ego inflating lines such as "We are this and we are also that, we've done this and we've achieved that." This is all guff and the buyer doesn't care a hoot. I really do not give a crap what you think you are, what's in it for me?

Instead of that, try thinking this way.

What do you want your "ideal customer" to think and feel when they think of your business? - Once you have narrowed down your ideal customer, the one where the highest profit margin is, or where the least amount of service is required, (both is best) you can really get into understanding what drives them and start working on your branding.

FALMOUTH BOAT HIRE QUALITIES

You saw within our strategic objective that I set out a mission for Falmouth Boat Hire that was simple and very much tied in with our target customer:

"The highest quality and longest standing boat hire company in Cornwall".

People generally accept there is a price to pay for the best, so I wanted to be the best, and charge for it. If you go in with low prices there is a low expectation, and it is very hard to push things upwards.

With regards to "longest standing" I wanted us all to understand we were not a just another pop-up tourist service trying to cash in - there was history, there was tradition, there was experience, there was credibility. The team believed this too.

RESEARCH WHO YOUR IDEAL CUSTOMER IS

When it comes to working out your ideal customer much can be done by researching. You almost need to work out a profile of them. These are the sort of questions you can write down and start trying to work out.

- Are they family people with disposable income?
- Are they young single people?
- Are they mature or retired looking for exclusivity?
- Are they women interested in parenting?
- Are they men looking for exhilaration?

Get a pen and some paper, or open your laptop and start writing down these questions, and then start trying to find answers to them for your own business. Again it is important to focus. You cannot be everything to all people, it is impossible, find the profile of that "ideal customer".

FALMOUTH BOAT HIRE'S IDEAL CUSTOMER

This was the ideal customer for us right here.

A caring family looking to give their children a wonderful experience.

What sort of parents does that conjure up in your mind? Think about it. A family such as this is most definitely not looking for thrills. The father is looking for a calm adventure and the mother a safe healthy lifestyle experience for her children.

A family like this will pay for a quality lifestyle experience that is "safe family fun" (one of our marketing taglines in fact). I know this profile well because it fits me, it is exactly what I want for my own family.

Quite often you'll find that the person in charge of the business will choose a business or product offering that resonates with them personally. What is yours? I'm not suggesting you can't build, brand and market a business that doesn't resonate with you, but it sure as hell does help if you fully understand your ideal customer, emotionally. You can put yourself in their shoes.

This family profile also proved time and time again to be conscientious and needed the least amount of supervision and would treat our boats with due care. They are responsible people that are safe in a boat, my boats!

GET A COOL LOGO AND COLOUR SCHEME

You don't need to overthink this, I certainly didn't.

I went out to a local graphic designer and explained our strategic objective, our values, our ideal customer and tradition.

Good graphic designers should be able to translate this into a great visual for you.

This is important.

Use it everywhere and religiously.

I would also avoid common mistakes like using the first letter of each word and creating a logo reading FBH. FBH would mean everything to me but may as well be Greek to anyone else, it simply has no use or value. So avoid that, its crap and will also do you no favours in search engine marketing. More on that later.

WHAT KEY MESSAGES DO YOU WANT TO CONVEY?

Write these down, they should come directly from your Strategic Objective.

As I said all your staff should be on board with the business Strategic Objective, and they should also be familiar with the branding/marketing messages.

You should write up cards with your key messages on and laminate them handing them out to your staff. Get them to learn them by heart.

Your staff form an important part of customer touch points, they totally represent your brand, it is your responsibility to ensure they convey your key messages consistently and repeatedly.

WHAT ARE YOUR KEY MARKETING MESSAGES?

As I said our ideal customer was *"A caring family looking to give their children a wonderful experience."*

Therefore our key marketing messages became such things as:

- Safe family fun
- Best experience of our holiday
- Healthy outdoor family time
- Wildlife viewing potential
- Stunning picturesque and tranquil experiences

These were used throughout various marketing collateral we developed. Not only did I use them throughout our collateral I would even repeat the key messages when responding to TripAdvisor reviews, or emails. You should do the same.

DO YOU INTEGRATE YOUR KEY MARKETING MESSAGES?

You'll hear me talk about communication touch points.

This basically means every time your business interacts with a customer, think:

- Telephone
- TripAdvisor
- Email
- Invoices
- Facebook
- Face to face communication

Every time a member of staff interacts with a customer they are communicating your branding, they are marketing for the business, they are a vital component in the chain.

We made sure all staff were on board with integrating the brand identity.

Every message we wrote on social media, every time we answered the phone it was consistent. The same tone, the same phrases, the same experience.

The customer was put front and centre and made to feel special every single time.

Periodically I would do fake hire run-throughs to check the staff were communicating correctly and effectively.

WHAT IS THE TONE OF VOICE OF YOUR BUSINESS?

Communication can be an art form. When developing a business tone of voice it is my advice to talk in the language that is going to appeal to your ideal customer.

Is your business tone one or none of these?

- Snazzy?
- Vibrant?
- Energetic?
- Risky?
- Aggressive?

If you are trying to communicate a calm tranquil family experience you cannot answer the phone with any of the tones above.

If however you were trying to market your adrenaline lifestyle experience business all would be a good choice.

OUR TONE OF VOICE

Falmouth Boat Hire's tone of voice was one of reassurance, confidence, calmness, positivity and belief.

We had true belief we were the highest quality and longest standing boat hire company in Cornwall - and you know what, we did indeed become it soon enough!

Every phone call had to convey this, even when we were really were stressed or rushed.

I didn't want a single customer leaving a phone call thinking "damn those guys are stressed out and rude" or anything remotely similar, it was not fitting with the branding. One pissed off customer will certainly tell their friends, that goes on social media and you can come unstuck very easily.

GET A BUSINESS TAGLINE

Write these down, a list of things that capture the essence of your business.

Single short sentences are best.

Try to make them emotive, one of my favourites for FBH was "safe family fun" - this is immediately attractive to the parents and completely excluding to the stag parties.

TAGLINE EXAMPLES

- MasterCard: "There are some things money can't buy. For everything else, there's MasterCard."
- BMW: "The Ultimate Driving Machine"
- Tesco: "Every Little Helps"
- Dunkin' Donuts: "America Runs on Dunkin"
- The New York Times: "All the News That's Fit to Print"
- Maybelline: "Maybe she's born with it. Maybe it's Maybelline."

You don't need to have just one, you can use a variety of them in different advertisements or literature. We mainly stuck with Safe Family Fun though, it works very well for us across the board. And you know what? We stopped getting requests for stag parties very quickly.

THINK ABOUT TEMPLATES

Everything you design and use you can template.

- Invoices
- Email signatures
- Colour schemes
- Product colours
- Uniforms
- Giveaways

Consistency is key with templates, or any form of business material. You don't get random coloured cups of coffee in Costa you get consistent branding every time. Just because your business is not Costa doesn't mean you can't think the same way, you can and should.

A CUTE STORY AROUND BRANDING AND COLOURS

Historically Sunfleet boats were red and Moonfleet were blue, which was a sensible choice back in the day as they were two different independent businesses run by two different sets of people. The two businesses had differentiation. However, over the years the two fleets amalgamated and became one, the business bought by Chas in fact. He bought Sunfleet and Moonfleet as a single business.

Then when we changed to Falmouth Boat Hire, the concept of Sunfleet and Moonfleet was no longer relevant. We had mainly blue boats with a couple of reds ones, it was all very inconsistent and I pushed hard each year, and harder the next year to rid Chas of hanging on to the red boats. He would fight back, resisting my pleas to go all blue and be consistent with the branding and colours.

You know what happened?

The last year we traded we left the one remaining red boat out of the water, and guess what? A buyer approached us!

It makes me chuckle now, a coincidence I am sure, but amusing for me nonetheless. Told you Chas! :)

BE TRUE TO YOUR BRANDING

Customers will keep coming back to you if you are true to your branding.

You go back to Apple and Nike, Coca-Cola for these reasons, consistency.

Of course you may not be after repeat customers, but even so if your branding and communication is consistent throughout their experience they will feel comfortable.

For Falmouth Boat Hire I wanted to ensure the entire boat hire experience was branded consistently. This helped a great deal with TripAdvisor reviews and the recommendations to friends. No surprises for the customer, always consistent. If a customer came for a boat hire and got in a blue boat, they'd expect to get in a blue one the next time too.

Also red is a daring and aggressive colour, it's not associated with calmness. I'd urge you to do some research on the psychology of colour and the emotions that colours invoke in us, it's quite fascinating.

In summary this section asked you to consider how you want your business to look. Start from who your ideal customer is, not what you think you are. I'm sure you have an awesome service/product, but WHO will buy it, who do you want to buy it? Research that ideal customer, and start coming up with key messages that would interest them. With that done get a graphic designer to convey your research into a graphic and colour scheme.

Start templating and using this throughout every single communication touch point.

How will you build your business' reputation?

(How to attract customers in the digital age)

Who doesn't book services without reading online reviews these days? You may not understand it fully, but social media and search engines can make or break your business. This section will explain the importance of protecting your reputation, and will show you how to manage your engagement with the big platforms.

BRAND REPUTATION

Reputation is a concept that your business must pay close attention to, I certainly did with Falmouth Boat Hire. Though it was a small local business I thought about it like a big global player.

Good reputation is everything in the business world and especially so for small to medium size businesses, because often it is only you, and if you get a bad reputation you'll not be able to afford a top tier PR agency to fix it for you.

WHAT IS BRAND REPUTATION EXACTLY?

This seems obvious when written in black and white, but is it? Reputation according to the dictionary is:

"the opinion that people in general have about someone or something, or how much respect or admiration someone or something receives, based on past behaviour or character."

Put like that it seems a fairly easy thing to manage, and to an extent one could argue it is, when we are dealing with a singular person off-line, in the physical world, without the ability to rant or rave to others easily on social media.

This offline environment, the "closed-loop" was the game played by businesses for years. We only had to mainly concern ourselves with individuals and ensure they had a great customer experience or service. If the experience didn't live up to their expectations they may have told a few close friends but generally the bad reputation would have stopped there, unless mainstream press got hold of it.

It was generally only in a crisis situation when the mainstream newspapers got hold of a story and sensationalised it so that a business then suddenly had a large scale reputation issue on their hands. A PR firm would be called in and paid lots of money to fix it.

PR is not rocket science or black magic, it is much like flooding all available channels (depending on budget) with the spin you require to influence people with. PR people are paid to persuade. Often PR is blatant lies, or twisted truth, rhetorical and horseshit. That sounds a bit harsh, OK, so sometimes PR just exaggerates the good bits and does not mention the bad bits, or apologises for the client and gives a reason why. More on that later.

THEN CAME SOCIAL MEDIA

However, this has all changed, not the mass media, that's still strong, but the singular customer telling a few friends has changed, it has changed because now the singular customer will voice their opinions about a service received on their Facebook or Twitter account.

And you know what?

Issues can soon escalate out of control and your small to medium sized business can have a very big problem from a small hiccup.

Social networks are by default particularly adept at facilitating gossip, and the majority of us love a good rant and rave. It is often the extremes that get amplified, either positively or negatively. Do you even know if your business is being mentioned?

Added to this we all suffer from Herd Behaviour, in that if our friends start moaning and creating bad reputation about a brand, we are likely to "jump on the bandwagon" too, regardless of our experiences, to a point. This is a highly dangerous phenomena and scares the crap out of me if I'm honest.

With Falmouth Boat Hire if I noticed positive things being said I would often jump in and find a way of amplifying them even further. With negative sentiment I would try to take it offline and deal with it, I never ignored it.

5 SIMPLE STRATEGIES TO COPE

1. CREATE GOOD SERVICE

Naturally you should avoid creating bad reputation in the first place at all costs. This may sound like basic stuff but I am amazed daily by exceptionally bad customer service, be it a phone manner, or an employee, or the way a shop assistant talks to me.

Just this morning I was in Bristol airport, UK, getting a flight to Amsterdam, and for some reason I visited the disabled access washroom, I don't know why, it was the first door and I was busting. So I go to wash my hands and look at the sink, then the pipework, then the floor, then the mirror. Everything was filthy, a serious lack of attention to cleaning detail everywhere, very much a "could not care less" attitude.

I blame not the worker, but the boss, the manager for not putting in place excellence and standards to strive for and to ensure they are being met. Clearly a process what not in place. A process derived from a Strategic Objective that stated: "We will be the cleanest washrooms in any UK airport" or whatever.

The reason I was checking the place more than usual is that outside they have one of those smiley face voting machines, where you click the happy or sad button based on how clean they were. So of course I clicked the very sad face, it was terrible.

This is a classic case of bad reputation as I've now told you and if you ever visit the same airport you'll think about this story. There is simply no excuse for it, it's lazy and bad management.

If your business has great services and customers receive excellent products then your brand is unlikely to receive bad reputation, in fact it is likely to receive praise on-line!

2. MONITOR USING GOOGLE ALERTS

Google alerts is an excellent way of being notified when Google finds information you are monitoring. With Google Alerts you can set it up to monitor keywords and be told if and when those keywords are found on the Internet. Monitoring your brand name is essential at the bare minimum. You can also use Google Alerts to monitor your competitors, and tons of other very cool stuff. Let's say you like my book here and write a blog post about it. I'd get notified by Google if my name is found in the text of your blog post. Sweet eh? I used a lot of Google Alerts for keywords relating to Falmouth Boat Hire that might by typed into Google. I wanted to know what was being said and where. Where there opportunities for me? Has someone written a travel blog about "top ten things to do in Cornwall" - I wanted to know, because I wanted to tell them we should be included in the list. Things like this are valuable to grow your online presence.

3. MONITOR GOOGLE SEARCH ENGINE RESULTS PAGES (SERPS)

Everyone has Googled their own name surely? Though this seems glaringly obvious to some of us it is in fact not so obvious to all. This is something you should do on a fairly regular basis for your brand name and services. Keeping control of the front page of Google for your business is an essential activity. If you find bad reputation entries here it is time to consider some reputation management activities. As I said above I had Google Alerts to tell me whenever Google had found something relating to my business. If I found something I didn't like I would devise a plan to tackle it. This is beyond the scope of this book but I get into it with my online courses.

4. GOOGLE MAPS AND REVIEWS

Google also likes to pinpoint on a map every single business on the planet, and your small business is no exception. Even if you have not requested for it to be added, and created the map entry yourself it is likely someone would have already done this for you. Have you claimed it? Do you have access to edit the entry? You can claim your business listing quite easily by requesting Google to verify your business through Google Places (google.com/business). Google will verify your business either by sending you a letter with a code contained within, or a text message to your phone.

You really should have control of your own business entry on Google Maps so you can at the very least put across the key things you wish your business to be known for. In addition you should keep a close eye on the reviews for each entry. I've enjoyed posting some bad reviews myself for local businesses, a garage in one instance provided terribly bad service, and my review is there for the whole world to see. In fact others joined in on the rant. This of course appears #1 on Google for their brand search - not good! Maybe I should offer my services to fix it for them?

5. TWITTER KEYWORD MONITORING

Twitter is one place where gossip and ranting and raving is very much at home, this is where an ideology (be it positive or negative) can really get some traction. Every time I look at my Twitter stream I will see someone, or a collective of people, having a good old rant. It could be your business they are talking about! You do not have to be an active user of Twitter to monitor it, you don't have to take part in the conversation itself and spend hours each day creating tweets, but you DO need to be aware if your business is being talked about, and more importantly know what to do about it, if it is! I personally use Hootsuite and I set up columns where I monitor client keywords to ensure I'm always in on the conversation should one arise.

You can think of outsourcing your social media activity, but be very careful it usually best if it comes from within, only you and your team really know your business.

There are many strategies that you should be looking at, really, many, but these 5 are a great starting point for you.

TRIPADVISOR

I was not a TripAdvisor fan before I bought into Falmouth Boat Hire. In fact I despised it and couldn't see the value in the early years. If the business wasn't on the TripAdvisor site why should I open the door for public reviews? Believe me this naive perception changed swiftly when I experienced first-hand the benefits customer reviews could bring to my tourism-based business.

TripAdvisor receives a lot of a traffic, I mean a LOT! It fact it has become the defacto place for the large majority of tourists who want to get the scoop on local places, be it a seafood restaurant, boutique hotel and everything in between. I actually stumbled into adopting TripAdvisor for Falmouth Boat Hire. Actually that's not quite true I was rather pushed into using it as a customer went ahead and somehow created a review for us without us having a listing. This was an immediate, full awareness, and sobering red light that I had to get on board with it. If customers were starting to use it, for my business, I simply, had to get some control over it and work it to the business' advantage, just as you must. However, you have to get your business firing on full cylinders for it to work well for you, otherwise it will help sink you.

So having noticed a customer had reviewed the business with the listing unowned, or not claimed I went ahead and claimed it just like I did for the Google Maps entry. Once you've verified you are the business owner you are then able to access a variety of management tools and marketing assets. I then started to make the public page for the business look good with relevant images, persuasive text and marketing messages that were in tune with our Strategic Objective and value propositions. I then responded as the owner of the business and thanked the person for their review. It was actually a very good review, which ultimately made me want more and more of the same to use as a marketing channel.

Here is our first ever review.

"Fun on the Fal"

5 Stars Reviewed 17 July 2013 via mobile

This is without doubt the best way to spend a few hours around Falmouth.

Found on Custom House Quay, the operators are very nice to chat to and great to deal with.

The boats are not too big but will seat 6, not too fast but they are perfect for the area. You can explore the Fal, look around the docks, and even go out as far as Black rock for a spot of fishing.

The great thing is you can do as you please (within reason!) Rather than being tied to a pleasure boat itinerary.

It is great fun being the skipper of your own boat, they are very stable and you can cover good distance, we were surprised how far we got.

The first hour looks a touch pricey but you need two hours or more to get the best from the day at which point the costs is equal to or better than other hire boats in the county, but remember, this is not just a trip round the bay it is a proper explore trip!

There is no better way to explore the Carrick roads or the Fal (unless you own a boat).

Visited July 2013

What a fantastic start we had, I was sold. In fact it was so good I should have offered him a marketing job!

This then led me to developing a cunning plan, to actively develop TripAdvisor as a marketing channel for us.

Here's what I did. I had a couple of thousand postcards designed with nice images of our boats on them pictured in the sunset with simply the words 'Thank you for your business - here's a 10% coupon code for future boat bookings'.

I briefed all staff members that when they sensed the customer had a fabulous experience they should hand one of these postcards out with a warm smile. Then when the customer showed appreciation, kindly ask them if they would leave a review on TripAdvisor for us. This may sound like cherry picking and using TripAdvisor to our advantage, and of course it is!

We would still hand out thank you cards to customers that had a mediocre experience, for whatever reason, although we would not suggest they leave a half-hearted TripAdvisor review.

The fact is we were very fortunate because our boat experiences were really very good ones almost always.

As I said above, for TripAdvisor to work for you there is no hiding, you either make it your interest to be the best or you don't. I had no other thought in my mind than to be the best boat hire company in Cornwall, period. Every bit of attention to detail was all related back to that early Strategic Objective I wrote. I hope you are seeing the importance of that throughout the book.

WHAT TO DO WITH BAD REVIEWS

To be fair we didn't get many, I think two, possibly three. However, you have to be realistic and there will always be someone that is just impossible to please. Life is full of people that have nothing better to do than complain.

Here's what you do with a bad review. > DO NOT RESPOND ONLINE FIRST <

If you have the customer contact details dig it out and call them on the phone! This will be a very surprising phone call for the customer. You should have a plan about what you will say though, and be prepared. If you do not have a telephone number, you should try to email them.

USE THE 3 R'S OF CRISIS COMMUNICATIONS

Sounds a bit heavy? A bad review on TripAdvisor is not a time for crisis communications? Think again, it really is serious marketing collateral to pay attention to.

In the public relations and media industry for such things as crisis management there is a simple rule that is used that you can follow. It is called the three R's. These stand for:

1. Regret
2. Reason
3. Remedy

1. **Regret** - This is the first thing that is expressed. *"I am sincerely sorry for your bad experience with us, it really is not what we are all about. I wanted to speak with you personally to provide a sincere apology."*
2. **Reason** - Secondly you explain why this happened. *"Despite our very best efforts we simply didn't perform well here, and not to blame anyone we did suffer from a staff sickness and were short-handed. This is not the normal for us and typically we have a full complement of staff. As you can see your negative rating is in fact way outside of the normal 5 stars we receive repeatedly."*
3. **Remedy** - Lastly you explain what you will do to rectify it. *"We have made some changes in how we plan for staff illness and have also subscribed to a recruitment agency we can draw personnel from when needed. I want to extend my*

apology further and provide you with the option of another experience with us at no cost whatsoever, and we will also provide three coupons for discount for your friends."

There is one last thing you need to do.

You ask if that customer would reconsider their review in light of your conversation and remove the bad review from TripAdvisor. You explain the significance that TripAdvisor can have on a small business like yours, and how it can make or break a business. You do not beg here, you just clearly point out the adverse effect that can result from a negative rating.

Here is a real life conversation I had with a customer who left us a bad review. It was a justified review too. It was late season when we typically only trade if there is a booking. A booking did slip through the net due to a booking system error, and the poor customer was left waiting. Not good!! Here's how it went:

"Dear xxx

I just saw your TripAdvisor review and I was deeply saddened by this. I am extra sad due to it being on your boyfriend's birthday. I wanted to contact you personally as the Director to say sorry.

The reason this happened is not due to weather or us being lazy (as you stated), we actually pride ourselves on excellent customer service as you can see from all our 5 star reviews. The reason was simply due to a technical error and the booking not showing up in our system (our member of staff you spoke to didn't know this). We use a third party booking software and it simply failed to log your booking in our calendar. We have approached the company about this.

On behalf of Falmouth Boat Hire I would like to offer you and your boyfriend a free half day trip at a time convenient for you both (might have to be next year as the season is ending now). If you can't make it I can also offer a voucher for the same price that you could give to one of your friends.

You can rest assured we take customer service very seriously and have failed in this instance due to no fault of ours. I hope this apology and gift goes some way to helping the situation. If you would reconsider your TripAdvisor review it would be fantastic as for a small local business it's very damaging for us.

Yours sincerely,

Chris Hambly

Director

Falmouth Boat Hire

http://falmouthboathire.co.uk/"

The response:

"Hi Chris,

Thank you for your email,

I felt I had to write the review because the group were let down and upset. I understand it was due to a technical error however I had at least 2 emails confirming the booking, and it was sad that no one arrived to sort it out and apologise personally even when you were phoned.

We are very grateful of your offer of a free half day boat hire. Does the offer include our friends too? Do we need to book a date now?

Thank you for your offer and I'll look into amending the review."

And my response.

"Hi xxx

We feel so very bad about this, we really do, it is so unlike us. The emails are automated from the booking system, and we had no idea it was booked, therefore no idea they were sent.

Again, so very sorry.

Of course we are happy for you and your friends to have a free trip, it really is the least we can do, no problem at all.

It will have to be next season now - we typically start from Easter each year through to October half term.

You can just contact me when you would like to book and we will gladly offer you a coupon code that provides a 100% free booking on us.

We really appreciate you amending the review, it means so much to us.

Chris Hambly

Director

Falmouth Boat Hire

http://falmouthboathire.co.uk/"

And it worked, the customer did in fact remove the bad review.

My response was indeed very sincere, yours need to be too. You need to take a bad review personally and get to the bottom of why it happened, and attempt to never again let it be repeated.

You can see this type of three R's approach played out almost daily on TV news when a crisis hits. Take for example a gas boiler blowing up a house with resultant casualties. You will see trained personnel come onto the TV and use a very similar tactic of the three R's.

WHAT IF YOU HAVE TO RESPOND PUBLICALLY?

If you cannot contact the customer personally, you have no choice but to respond publically. However, you do this when you are relaxed and in a good frame of mind, certainly not angry, or worse, drunk!

You answer professionally and you craft your message using the crisis communication method of the three R's. When a customer is factually incorrect you also indicate that they are incorrect and state what is in fact true. However, try to phrase your answer so that you are not opening up an argument, or a chance for them to repeatedly come back, you need closure on that review as soon as possible. If the bad review can't be taken away you need other potential customers to see you do care, and that you really do give a crap about your customers' opinions.

It's hard to take it on the chin, but you will. Feeling these things personally is unavoidable because your business is your baby and the buck stops with you, nobody else. Take them as further learning experiences and challenges to up your game.

TIP: If you can turn a negative customer into a positive repeat one they will become the best customer you ever have.

In summary this section dealt with how you can build your brand's awareness. We looked at defining what branding is, and how social media cannot be ignored. I talked about the importance of being aware of what is being said about your business online and how you can monitor yours. We then looked at the power of

TripAdvisor and what you can do to utilise it as a marketing platform, and reputation tool. We live in the digital age, ignore it at

How will you reach more customers?

(What kind of business doesn't have a website these days?)

Falmouth Boat Hire needed a marketing strategy and so does every business, and a website very much forms part of that strategy. A business website in this day and age is essential, and I would argue it is essential in all sectors, absolutely every one of them, I can't think of a single business that would not benefit from one. Getting a website does not have to be expensive at all. You may well be approached by "web designers" who will charge you thousands and thousands of pounds for "website design" that will be as much use to you as a chocolate teapot. This section will focus on what you should and should not do when creating your website, and how to make your website stand out from the crowd.

THE GREAT WEB DESIGN HOAX

In an age where the Internet is considered the most reliable source of relevant information, businesses, both big and small, are responding to this fact by making sure that their online presence does not only generate traffic, but that website visits translate into a sale or signup for a service (an outcome or action). It's interesting that one of the very first things that a company considers regarding websites is "design".

People will often search for "website design" or "website designers". It seems this is programmed into the psyche of so many people where they think that design is the most important facet of a website – let me tell you this, it isn't! A better search would be "website engineer" or "search engine optimisation specialist" or "internet traffic specialist" - anything but a "designer". Most designers just make things look pretty, might be harsh, but that's my experience. Let me tell you that a website with no traffic is useless, pointless, a fat waste of cash, and no matter how amazing it looks.

Falmouth Boat Hire's website was designed solely for traffic generation and traffic conversion, nothing else.

OK, sure design plays a part of an overall strategy, but it's only one quarter at best, and in fact can be even far less than that depending on the purpose of the website.

It can be intimidating to build a website but with a good web engineer and by paying attention to the following three key elements your website will have an impact.

1. SEARCH ENGINE OPTIMIZATION

Getting your website seen is far more important than how it looks. It has become a priority that your website must come on the first few pages of search results. Did you know that the top 5 URLs (links) on the search engine results pages (SERPs) get 75% of user clicks. Search and email are the top two Internet activities.

It starts by coming up with the right content. By picking out the right keywords, your website(s) can stand out in search results and potential customers can start finding your business.

Having the right kind of content that is reliable and consistently updated will make visitors come back because it makes Google interested. Google just wants to present the most relevant search results to users, so you have to make sure your site has content to aid that.

This is the single most important lesson to extract from me in this book...

BUILD A SITE OPTIMISED FOR WHAT GOOGLE IS LOOKING FOR, BASED ON WHAT PEOPLE TYPE INTO SEARCH

With traffic you can do stuff, without traffic you can do nothing.

Traffic can lead to an email subscription, a participation in a survey, or even a sale; either way, the website visit has generated action from the target audience that is beyond reading the content. The website call to action for FBH was either a telephone call to book a boat or a direct booking through our online booking system, which was the absolute best outcome.

I've written a larger section below about SEO that you can read shortly, it's VERY important. I'll also touch on how you can install a website quickly yourself later in this book.

2. USER EXPERIENCE

With more Internet users owning smartphones and tablets, it is equally important for them to be able to browse their favourite websites through these gadgets. For website visitors, it enhances their user experience when they can see through their mobile phone or tablet exactly what they see when they are browsing through their personal computers. Moreover, an fancy web design loses its touch when visitors get lost in navigating through the page.

Regardless of how attractive the web page is, if the user cannot get the information he needs because he cannot navigate through the website, it defeats the purpose of having a well-designed website. I will explain in the next section why having a mobile-friendly website is so important. We got a lot of great feedback for the FBH website, due mainly to its simplicity. Everything was laid out to funnel people to what we wanted.

I apply the K.I.S.S. formula to websites. Keep It Simple Stupid.

3. COPY WRITING

With well researched and carefully selected keywords, your website will generate traffic. At times, having the right content material is half the task. Information must also be presented in an organised and cohesive manner to help your readers to understand exactly what you are communicating. The choice and organisation of words contribute to effective copywriting. No matter how accurate the information is, if the readers experiences a hard time to understand it, a website would definitely have a challenge in retaining its audience and probably will not convert viewers into customers very well.

A well-designed simple website is indeed an effective marketing strategy. However, the real challenge lies on how to keep visitors coming back, referring it to their peers, and actually taking an action on what they have viewed or read. This is where the above mentioned factors come in and contribute to the success of a marketing strategy.

So don't be fooled by the great website design hoax, get something that is joined-up!

IF YOUR WEBSITE DOESN'T WORK ON A PHONE YOU ARE SETTING FIRE TO CASH

Since 1991, we have seen the internet grow almost exponentially and the number of websites that now populate it is evidence of that unprecedented growth. As an example of this, there was only a single website in 1991 when it all started. By 1997, that figure had grown to 1,000,000. Only 10 years later (2007), there were 150 million websites. There are now over 1 billion websites today – and growing. Google estimates that the Internet now contains roughly five million terabytes of data – but the search giant has indexed only 0.04% of it all.

As smartphones are the norm websites are often viewed on mobile devices. Mobile-friendly websites are compatible with (you guessed it) mobile devices such laptops, smartphones, and tablets. 50% of search users begin their search with a mobile device and this percentage will only increase. It's not a question of asking if a mobile friendly website is important, we know this, the question becomes is yours mobile friendly?

So what does this mean for the small business owner who has a website that isn't mobile-friendly? It means you could be burning money in the form of lost revenues. To illustrate its importance, here are 5 factors to consider about being mobile-friendly:

1. **Better brand engagement** – Statistics have shown that consumers tend to like a particular brand more if they can

purchase it over their mobile devices. Additionally, they are more likely going to visit your site again.

2. **Increased sales conversions** – Calls to Action (CTAs) should be readily visible and simple to click on. This is the problem with seeing a regular desktop website in a mobile browser – they are ineffective for converting visitor traffic to sales because CTAs may be obscured and it may be difficult to click on the link. A CTA doesn't have to be complicated it is merely something you want the user to do. Sign up for a newsletter, call you on the phone, navigate to another page etc. Do always have a CTA. As mentioned before I always wanted a boat booking, or at the very least a telephone call to in inquire about booking a boat.

3. **Mobile consumers are different** – Their objectives are different from those of desktop users in that they are searching for information and they want it quickly. Their buying habits tend to differ as well. Speed really is the essence, fast access, workable.

4. **Mobile-friendly websites get plenty of visitor traffic** – 50% and increasing daily of all global searches are now being done on mobile devices and that might just equate to a serious increase in sales.

5. **Mobile users are in a hurry** – Your website content on a desktop may be readable but on a mobile device, it won't

be. When this happens, visitors bounce. In other words, they move on to another site. Either way, you lose. In website analytics we talk of the Bounce Rate and you want a low Bounce Rate. High Bounce Rates will also not aid your SEO efforts, Google understands a Bounce Rate and it forms part of the Google ranking algorithm.

Your website must be responsive and mobile ready. A responsive website means it responds to whatever screen size it is viewed on. That is to say, it dynamically adjusts itself. DO NOT get fleeced into paying for two versions, you need one site that works on all devices. Falmouth Boat Hire obtained the **majority** of its sales through users on a mobile device. I could tell this by looking at website analytics and seeing what browser/device was used.

If you think for a minute about the type of customer we had you can understand that many tourists do not travel with a laptop anymore, they just take the phone. Seeing as our target audience was primarily tourists it's pretty easy to understand how our main player was mobile.

CONTENT MANAGEMENT

Content marketing is without a doubt one of the best ways to promote your website. I published a lot of material relating to boats, Falmouth and the surrounding area.

When I refer to content marketing I mean regularly publishing a new article/news/tutorial/ on your website. <u>One specific article for each search term you are chasing</u>.

I wrote unique articles with titles such as:

- Boats For Rent In Cornwall
- Boat For Tall Ships Falmouth
- Hire A Boat In Cornwall
- Things To Do In Falmouth
- Cornwall Boat

The list goes on and on and on…. And on and on and on. The thing is that each one of these articles become a unique link in Google, each one is specific to a search term someone may type into Google. Lots more on this in the SEO section later.

There are some general things you can consider when creating content. The following are some simple tips I used to ensure that content marketing was a valuable endeavour, for both the business and our customers.

1. CREATE HYPE

Readers are not looking for old news or outdated information that is only focused on promotion. It pays off to follow industry trends, and offer quality insights that may be related to your industry, even if not to your business specifically. By getting customers excited about other possibilities that your company is a part of, they will value this information, and remember that you supplied it.

2. HIGHLIGHT TRENDS

This is related to creating hype, but goes further as to show different ways that your products and services may be utilised to replicate current style, design, and lifestyle benefits that are in the news. By keeping your clients up to date with what is happening in the world, you are also showing them that your business is current and cutting-edge. I really worked the healthy lifestyle trend into Falmouth Boat Hire's messaging. Think about how you can mirror trends in your messaging.

3. ADD VALUE

Ensure that your content provides something that is unique. This can include industry information, facts, or even just answering "how to" questions about products and applications. Your added value will be that your content is a resource, not just for your business, but also for customers who are looking for answers. Adding value about Falmouth was pretty simple as I live in Falmouth and know the area very well, so pointing to interesting articles about what to see and do in Falmouth helped add value.

4. PROVIDE INTRIGUE

This can come from interviews with other professionals, or with audio visual snippets such as casts and demonstration videos. Altering your content between text and visual media will keep clients coming back to see what you are offering next. Definitely use video, I'll get into video shortly. Try to add a little mystery about your business. Is there a story you can tell?

5. TEACH

Educating your customers will be a great benefit, as not only will they come to see your content as a valuable resource tool, they will also get the sense that your postings are unbiased, and for the general benefit. This builds both trust and reputation, and will establish you as a leader in your industry. Trust is really important for Google, really very important. I'm a huge fan of educating customers, in any industry. Education will set your business apart from your competitors. If you can be the one in your niche that people come to for information you are on to a huge win.

6. BE HUMAN

Often, this is accomplished with the way you write and gives you a way to connect with your customers. This allows for a common ground of shared experiences and both pitfalls and victories that happen along the way. Being human is a wonderful way to establish integration with your customer base.

7. INCLUDE YOUR CUSTOMERS

Allow your customers to submit content. Highlight your customers in your own content. This builds your business and your online community, and shows that you pay attention to details, and value the customers who support what you do. Perhaps you have case studies you can talk about. If you have case studies about people that are also active on the Internet as content writers it's a huge win and they will not be able to help themselves but share your stories about them.

Generating content can take time, it can seem daunting at first but once you get into a pattern it becomes just another one of those business processes that needs to be done to work "on" your business. You can even outsource content writing to a third party, there is an entire industry that meets this need. If you do it yourself my advice is to simply create a business process such as every Friday you will write one more piece of content during one hour of time, after a month you have four new articles that Google will be indexing.

In summary this section looked at the importance of a website for all businesses and indeed mobile friendly websites are now the normal. We also considered that a "web designer" should not be the way to think, but rather a "search engineer" is more appropriate. Content marketing is a vital component of a marketing strategy and you should make this a business process.

How will your business make it to number one?

(How often do you go to page two of the search results?)

Let's face it, when you want to know something you Google it, right? And you always click on the most relevant-looking result in the top three, right? Well it's no coincidence that those results are there - Google has algorithms to ensure you get the most relevant results based on your search. This section will explain how to harness the power of the Google search, and how to put yourself on the map

SEARCH ENGINE OPTIMISATION (SEO)

I need to come clean on this one and explain that I am somewhat of an expert when it comes to search engine optimisation.

Here's the thing.

My first business was an Internet based business, a virtual school in fact. What started out as the thesis for a Masters I was studying, in the subject area of Open and Distance Education, became a fully-fledged online business.

The business was known as Audiocourses.com (it no longer exists on that domain). Audiocourses.com offered a variety of courses to students that wanted to learn about music technology and sound engineering, you know, making records. Over a period of eight years the school enrolled students from every corner of the World and had a membership base of over 30,000 members at its most active point.

I can still remember when I built the first website and what was required for it to succeed. Internet traffic, and lots of it, was the vital component.

CONVERSION RATES

The thing is with ecommerce, of any kind in almost all industries, is that conversion rates are dreadfully low.

The term conversion rate is a measure, or rather a ratio, between the number of visits to an online shop and the corresponding number of purchases made. Plainly put, if 100 people visit your online shop and 5 of those 100 buy something from you, your store has a 5% conversion rate.

Let me tell you that if you do have a conversion rate of 5% you should continue to push hard on that channel because you are doing excellently. The fact of the matter is that the average ecommerce conversion rate is just a mere 1.33%. So for every 100 visitors about 1.5 will make a purchase!

Your business may not have an online shop, although the reason I am informing you about conversion rates is that your website must have a point to it. In digital marketing we generally call this a "goal". For you this may be that the customer calls your telephone number, fills in an online form to send you an email, downloads a free guide, etc. The point is, your website has a primary purpose, and generally this should be lead generation. For Falmouth Boat Hire the goal was very clearly aimed at encouraging the customer to make (and pay) for a booking through our online booking system. The secondary purpose of Falmouth Boat Hire's website was to provide information about the product for sale, the boat hire. However, all of those features were of course all about persuading the user to book a boat, plain and simple.

With a goal, a desired outcome, I could therefore work out my conversion rate. If a customer booked a boat through the online booking system, I would have an xyz conversion rate for bookings. If a user called the phone I would have an abc conversion rate for phone calls. The point here is there exists measurability, and without it, you are in the dark, so this should most definitely be on your checklist.

So then if conversion rates matter, and they really do, it stands to reason that most websites need a LOT of traffic to obtain a goal (successful Call To Action).

GOOGLE LOVES CONTENT

So back to my first business Audiocourses.com. I discovered very quickly that the key to rising up through the ranks of Google was to become an authority in my niche. Google needed to see my website as the best place to go for all things relating to "audio courses". This tied in very nicely with the domain itself, being audiocourses.com I already had two very relevant keywords not only in my title but also all over the site and contained in web links pointing back to my site (incoming links). Incoming links are also another vital indicator of a website's authority in Google's eyes.

As well as incoming links, which I will talk about in more detail later, I realised that for every new article I posted it would become one more unique url (uniform resource locator - or web link if you like) in Google's search engine results page. This is golden information. We are talking 2000/2001 here and even today in 2017 it amazes me that still the large majority of business websites do not do this. Why, is it lack of understanding? Too busy? Too lazy?

Make no mistake for every new article you post on your website, it really is another unique link in Google that potential customers can find your services for. What tends to happen is that website designers typically know very little about SEO, in fact some know absolutely nothing about it. Therefore, a website can be designed without a goal in mind. The website gets made to look pretty with lots of bells and whistles, and actually nothing happens, nobody sees it, plain useless. Do not let this be you. What you need to have is a content management system such as Wordpress which allows you to publish regular content. This is the case if you are using SEO as a channel for traffic. SEO is not the only way, we will look at other channels too, but SEO is generally long lasting and no budget required other than time to write and publish of course, which is a cost too.

So I learnt early on how to play the Google game with SEO, or Content Marketing, and the more I published every day the more traffic I saw coming in. So in essence audiocourses.com become a publishing site, as well as being a school. This was an excellent lesson to learn and I have adopted that with the majority of my online ventures ever since.

Tip: Get a content management system like Wordpress and publish content regularly.

GOING LOCAL DOWN IN ACAPULCO

Excuse the song reference but if you are running a local small business you'd be surprised at how easy it is to rank well in your market using the above SEO strategy. Let me give you a very real example of a client of mine.

Danny came to me asking about websites, he'd heard through George (who runs the fishing trips on the Quay) that I build websites and people's phones ring as a result of those websites.

Danny is a plasterer, you know, the inside and outside surfaces of houses, ceilings, wall insulation etc. So Danny popped into our Falmouth Boat Hire office (a van at the time) and started asking me if I could do something.

This is how it went.

Me: *"So Danny you want to attract people that are looking for a plasterer in Falmouth/Cornwall?"*

Danny: *"Yes, mate"*.

Me: *"So no disrespect Danny but you can't have a website called Danny Cole Plastering because nobody searches for Danny Cole Plastering."*

Danny: *"How do you mean?"*

Me: *"Danny, the thing is people will be carrying out searches for things like 'plastering in Falmouth' or 'plasterer in Cornwall' or 'Falmouth based plasterer'. And you should build out your business from that if you want to use Google."*

Danny: *"Really? But people know me as Danny Cole"*

Me: *"Danny, is your phone ringing? Only word of mouth will come to you from people knowing you, what about all the people using Google all the time these days, on their phones?"*

Danny: *"OK I get it, so that's what you have done with Falmouth Boat Hire, and George's website too?"*

Me: *"Exactly, I have started from what Google wants, or rather what people are searching for and built from there, to provide exactly that".*

Danny: *"That's smart man, can you do it for me?"*

Me: *"Of course, give me a week or two".*

And that was that, I registered the domain of cornwallplasterers.com and told him to publish content of his jobs including the location, this is important, the location bit. So I gave some examples of how to format the posts and what type of title to use.

Titles like these became posts:

- Cornwall Plasterers in Falmouth
- Falmouth Plasterer Completes New Walls
- Plastering Job Completed in Penryn

Etc..

For each of these posts, a unique link appears in Google. And considering none of his competition use this strategy he is now ranking number one for nearly all of the search terms he needs, to keep an endless supply of new clients calling. Danny even went on to rebrand his van with Cornwall Plasterers across the side, on my advice.

I have done this for countless local businesses, this is just one example. Falmouth Boat Hire is another.

You can do this for your own local business very easily. Chances are your competitors are not doing it. You also don't have to see a website as THE website, why don't you have three or four and treat each as a unique marketing channel?

Websites are very cost effective.

GOOGLE MAPS

Another part of the SEO puzzle is getting your local business on Google Maps, which I mentioned earlier. These listings only show when a location is identified in the search. These entries take up huge real estate on the search pages and are impossible to miss.

Part of the secret sauce here is to make sure your business details are 100% accurate. That is to say the web address, the actual real address (which has to be verified), the phone number etc all match up with what is on your site. I also believe they use other references too, so make sure that all your business lists wherever they are published are identical.

This was a challenge for Falmouth Boat Hire as for the first years I came on board we didn't have an operating office. The office was in fact a van, parked on the quay. We couldn't use my home or Chas's home address, otherwise customers may well be turning up there wondering where their boat was!

As a temporary solution we used a local art gallery on the Quay which was a mere 100ft from our "office". After a while we obtained a permanent office, which was actually a garden shed, but still it enabled me to call the address Falmouth Boat Hire, Suite 2, Custom House Quay, Falmouth, TR11 3JT, Cornwall, UK. I then edited the Google Maps marker to be in the exact location of the shed.

You might need to be creative if your local business shares an address with other businesses, for example shared office space, or multiple offices in the same building.

INBOUND LINKS

Inbound links are nothing more than links on other websites that link to your website. Google considers these an important ranking indicator that your site must be an authority. It's a great concept that Google came up with there. Think about it for a moment. Google is saying that the more inbound links your website has the higher the chances are that your website must be of significant value. It's kind of like crowd-sourcing really, where the public are doing the voting.

Not all inbound links are equal though.

When a user creates a web link on a website they do one of two things.

1. Paste the link in, like http://google.com
2. Link actual words, known as anchor text, like this.

In Google's algorithm the latter is by far the best as not only is a link being created but the link also now has context, a meaning, a subject.

Now this goes back to my argument of why having a website domain with the keywords of your services makes sense. You see when I started getting inbound links back to falmouthboathire.co.uk the anchor text used was 'Falmouth Boat Hire'. You can see this was perfect for my products. If the anchor text was 'Chris's Boats' linking to chrissboats.com the value would be low, as nobody searches for 'Chris's Boats'.

TIP: Leave your ego at the door regarding names and domains, give Google what it wants - what people search for.

OBTAINING INBOUND LINKS

There are two ways that inbound links can be obtained:

1. Natural process of other website owners linking to your content
2. Personally asking other website owners if they would link to your website

Number 1 is great because it means the content you have on your website is genuinely worth linking to. This occurred for Falmouth Boat Hire because other tourism-based operators linked to us as they felt their own customers would be interested in our service.

Number 2 happens because I personally sent other businesses emails asking if they would be kind enough to, because I felt their customers would be interested in our services. Also as strategic partnerships were being established I made it clear that a web link would be part of the deal. This is a good plan because if you are forming a strategic partnership with a business that has a website that Google thinks is an authority in their niche it will carry far more weight than a random newly formed website that has no authority yet.

It's quite easy to reciprocate too. You only have to have a page on your website that lists the partners. For Falmouth Boat Hire I started doing this for accommodation providers in the area. This yielded the result that we obtained authority through links of accommodation providers for Falmouth and the surrounding area, thus gaining more weight as being important for the term 'Falmouth' and in the tourism sector.

In addition, obtaining links from websites such as National Maritime Museums and Marine Directories we again garnered further authority in those niches.

TIP: You can do all of this in your niche, simply make a list of business that rank well in similar searches to your products, and then go and ask people for a link.

WHICH PLATFORM?

I can tell you now that I can build you a website for your target keyword, structured for future search optimised publishing in one hour. Think I'm joking? I've done it countless times for clients, that now rank #1 for their target keywords. The simpler the "design" the better. Google has started penalising sites that are overly complex in design because Google wants fast loading sites that work fabulously on a mobile phone.

Why am I telling you this? I am telling you this because I want you to not be a part of the web design fraud that takes place.

I've written a whole course about this, so it's beyond the scope of this book but what I will say is that all you need is Wordpress.

Wordpress is a content management system (CMS). This means you can publish content regularly, and you should. Most web hosts come with a one click install button to get the Wordpress framework installed on your domain. Wordpress can then be easily templated and structured for good SEO.

INTERACTIVE MAP

Falmouth Boat Hire still uses one of the hand drawn maps of the river. This must have been drawn back in the 60s. The map highlights the areas that are "no-go" on the river due to mud and where there are rocks or things to watch out for, it actually looks a lot like a pirate's treasure map, old world looking, hand drawn.

This map is still useful to point at and explain to customers the key points they need to know. We also had a waterproof copy of the map on board each boat. It's a tool that is designed to be used when talking to a customer, pointing and explaining places to stop etc.

On the website this map looked plain ridiculous. "Come on a boat hire and use this pirate treasure map" - not good.

Having experience with Google, Geolocation and mapping technologies I knew the solution.

I created a map on Google Maps with interactive markers that when clicked would reveal information about the location. This was a fabulous tool for a customer to click on during their time on our website. They could understand the places to visit and plan out the things they wanted to do whilst on the river. The more you can educate your potential customers with the benefits of your products the better.

TIP: You should think about ways to educate your customers with tools like this, edu-marketing if you like, teach them everything they need to know, inform them of the value, the potential.

VIDEO

Video is a powerful medium for selling your product

From the standpoint of marketing strategies and the promotion of products or services, videos have proven that they can be an extremely powerful selling tool. If you have yet to discover how video marketing can positively impact your sales, there are a number of reasons that you should consider integrating videos into your overall marketing strategies including:

- Video enables you to build trust among consumers while communicating in a more casual, conversational format.
- Video is appealing to the senses and engages a larger audience than other communication and marketing forms.
- Video provides you with a number of opportunities to demonstrate your products or services.

If a picture is worth a thousand words, how much do you think a promotional video would be worth – 10, 20, 100 times that? As a small business owner, you have enough on your plate so you're probably trying to figure out where you would find the time to produce a promotional video and then post it to your website. In this instance, you would be wise to hire a firm or development team to help you with your dilemma.

It's important to realise the advantages of using promotional videos as a selling medium. The following are some of the more compelling ones:

- It attracts and educates individuals that are visual learners.
- It builds the number of your search results.
- It effectively promotes the products or services you sell.
- It elevates your level of customer service and support.
- It harnesses the power of video platforms.
- It is a more personal form of advertising.
- It is cost-effective.
- It works!

Most internet marketers and online entrepreneurs are well aware of how promotional videos can be a very powerful selling tool. As was mentioned above, in addition to using videos for demonstrating how to use your products or services, you can use them for providing your customers with online support. More importantly, you can also record consumer testimonials and reduce the number of customer service calls and inquiries. I didn't capture customer testimonials directly but I did use customer footage in our videos.

Needless to say, all of these can eventually lead to increased sales and profits over the long term. The quality of the videos you create are equally as important as how you use them. You want to keep them short and directly to the point since individuals who browse and shop over the internet typically have short attention spans. The last thing you want to do is chase your prospective buyers off by using a long, boring video.

VIDEO AND YOUTUBE

YouTube is a good way to drive traffic to your website, as well as to host videos of your products and services, that you can embed into your website.

I had made a few videos of the boats on my mobile phone, the usual thing of boats coming and going, a few picturesque shots of the sunset etc. However, it was apparent we needed something more professional that would give the potential buyer a real sense of a boat hire experience.

I did a bit of snooping around on Twitter and noticed that a girl called Charlotte Dart was reasonably local to us and was advertising her services of producing a professionally shot and edited promotional video. She had some great examples on her website so I gave her a call.

Charlotte was a young girl just out of university, full of enthusiasm, and was making a go of freelancing with her boyfriend who was the techy one. They've since gone into drone recording and do very well at it. My next step for video would definitely have been a drone shot video of the boats up the river.

Charlotte turned up on a perfect day, it was beautifully still, delightfully sunny and was the absolute perfect conditions to shoot a video about boat hire. We had made a plan that I'd take her out in our uber fast rescue boat so that we could get to places up and down the river really quickly, she could then capture plenty of footage.

Being such a great day all of our boats were also out and dotted around the river which made for fantastic footage of customers enjoying their experience. Truth is that as we approached some of the customers in our rescue boat, clearly branded with Falmouth Boat Hire, waving a professional camera about, they actually started posing and putting on big smiles and a show for us, fabulous result.

Charlotte took the footage away, edited it and added a generic sound track, the result was perfect. We had a professionally made video that really did capture some of the highlights of our boat experiences. I had shared our key messages with Charlotte, our branding straplines and emphasised our ideal target customer. The video highlights the tranquillity of the river, the wildlife spotted, the ease of use, safe family fun, majestic scenery and a wonderful healthy day out, all branded with our logo, colours, font and messaging.

I put this video on our website and watched the views roll in. Not only did our conversion rate increase, but we also noticed people making comments about the video and how it really helped them make a decision to book a boat.

TIP: Don't underestimate the power of a professionally shot and produced video.

RE-USING YOUR ASSETS

I didn't stop at using the video on just the website, I also went to work on using it for our Facebook page, YouTube and Twitter.

It's important to maximise your investment as much as possible, really think about where you can use your advertising assets in as many advertising channels as possible. When I shared the video within our Facebook page we received a ton of shares from local people. I think this was down to the fact that local people are actually fiercely proud of where they live and the gorgeous environment. For these local people the video was just another justification of this truth, reinforcing their belief.

Twitter was much the same, I shared the video though a Falmouth Boat Hire Twitter account we had and copied in some Cornwall related tourisms accounts, that then went on and shared the video for us. Though to be honest a lot of that was just Cornwall-centric accounts and certainly not tourists so much, but still helped the business-to-business angle, which is also very important. You do want other businesses referring your business as much as possible, word of mouth is a very strong influence in a customer buying.

YOUTUBE AND SEO

What I will say about YouTube is this. Do not just upload your video and hope people will find it. You have to do some work to optimise a few things so that it matches up to the searches people are typing in. YouTube is just a search engine for video, so why would you not optimise your video for this too?

If I am honest one of the primary reasons for getting our promotional video created was to target YouTube for the primary search terms that customers use to find us through regular Google search.

You should always do a few things with YouTube...well any search-based channel really.

1. Search for your business name
2. Search for your key target keywords

It turned out that both of these turned up nothing for us, nothing, nada, zero.. This was a very good thing, it meant we could fix it, and fix it well, and we have no competition to beat.

HOW TO OPTIMISE YOUR YOUTUBE VIDEO

Google is a little dumb. It will not really understand the content of your video, you know, the visuals of it, the meaning, what it is all about. So you have to get busy with text, and use lots of it.

The title is very important, so you can probably guess what I used for our boats? Yes, Falmouth Boat Hire.

Next up is the description, and here you can pretty much construct an essay. Don't just add a single line paragraph, write as much as you can, write a story about the product, the service. The more words you can use the better. Though again, just like SEO, keep each single video optimised for one search term, don't put all your eggs into the one basket, it will lose its relevancy in YouTube. If you have ten products, have one video per product and optimise each video title and description for each product. I appreciate there is a cost for that, but think that way if you can, short snappy, very focused subjects for each video.

Tags are also useful. For each video you can add tags that relate to the content, so fill your boots, tag the crap out of each video with relevant keywords, again, relating the tags to the title, and the description. You should make it your job to help YouTube (Google) rank your video for relevancy. Always remember that videos that are relevant to a search term rank above videos that are not.

Other things that help are views and comments, so get sharing your video within social media channels, actively seeking comments and thumbs up! If you can get some inbound links (remember them?) that will also help significantly. You could think about how you could approach some of your strategic partners with an offer, if they would embed your video on their website for you. Because some of our videos contained shots of our strategic partner's premises, from the waterfront, of course we made a big deal informing them that we are featuring it on our website!

Is there a gap in the market for an educational tutorial or lesson about your product? Are people searching for something that does not exist, that relates to your service? If you can find that you will find it to be highly valuable.

You can see that strategy played out a lot with perhaps trade guys laying flooring tiles or driveways. "How To" videos are very popular, and not only do they generate a ton of traffic, the person or business that created them often gets lots of referrals from them.

Of course we became number 1 and 2 in YouTube for: "hire a boat in Falmouth".

TIP: Identify a gap in YouTube search which currently offers crappy and/or unrelated content. Fill that gap with your products/services.

GOOGLE ADWORDS

Google Adwords is a pay-per-click online advertising system. That is to say you create ads that google will display in various areas of its online real estate, the main one being Google search.

You will likely be familiar with these ads, they often appear at the top of the search results, and often in a sidebar too, always marked with a square box containing "A" in the corner of each ad.

As an advertiser you can choose to pay if someone goes ahead and clicks on your ad, or alternatively when someone just sees it. It's much like an auction where the higher the price you are prepared to pay the higher the position and more prominence your ad will have.

Google Adwords traffic is immediate, so once you switch the system on the traffic begins to flow, once you switch it off the traffic ceases. That is such an awesome business model Google have there.

This is pretty cool for a tourism-based business like Falmouth Boat Hire as a week or so before the season starts, or just before a big holiday we would switch the ads on and the phone would ring. It really was like turning on a tap and cash coming out.

With Google Adwords it is also very easy to target hundreds if not thousands of keyword combinations. When you start really researching and thinking about what the average customer might type into search you'll soon discover this huge long list of keyword phrases.

Google Adwords for us was a simple choice because only one other competitor in the area was using it for our main keywords/services. This meant the prices were low per actual click for us, and we could trump the competitor easily because we had a larger budget.

Tracking with Google Adwords, and being able to measure the return on investment is very simple. Because you know what you have spent on your ad campaign in say one week, you can actually track which ads drove customers to your website (through Google Analytics) and to a purchase. Google Analytics is free by the way and you must get that installed on your website, and start studying the reports.

It was a simple highly effective strategy, switch the ads on, the phone started ringing.

Because many of the more obscure keywords phrases we used had no competing ads, the prices were low. Coupled with this because you only pay when someone clicks on the ad so you can really fill up your keywords list with hundreds and hundreds of combinations.

Truth be told Google Adwords does not have a high click-through rate per search. That is to say people tend to favour clicking on the organic search results rather than the paid ads at the top of the page. Somehow we are consciously or unconsciously resistant to ads, so natural results through SEO will always convert better; but it makes no difference, if someone clicks and calls it's ker-ching, sale made, and if they don't click you don't pay!

This section really deserves far more detail but is beyond the scope of this book.

TIP: Always put the price of the product in the ad. Why? Well if a click is costing you money you need to give it every chance to convert a customer into a paying one. Making the cost explicit would prevent searchers that are priced out of the market from even clicking and costing you money.

In summary we considered some strategies to think about for helping your website get some serious prominence within Google. None are a magic bullet, some strategies are short, some are long, some cost more than others. The one thing that is important is that the all mostly link together in a joined up strategy. Much can be outsourced, much can be done within your business. The key takeaway is a website that works, attracts Google and becomes the main thrust of your marketing efforts.

Where should you spend your advertising money?

(Why bet on longshots when you can back the winner?)

We are constantly bombarded by advertisements these days, from overt TV and radio commercials, through peripheral ads on websites, billboards and posters, to subliminal product placement. Getting your message heard through all the noise is imperative, and luckily it's not as hard as you might think. This section explains how by simply paying attention to data you can stop betting on longshots and back the winner every time. From web advertising to local press, the value of every method can be measured.

Before I talk about advertising channels we used I want to be clear about one thing.

Capturing data for any form of marketing is pretty much a "no-brainer". If you do not know where your customers are seeing your business first, and therefore beginning to engage with your business, you have no idea if your ad spend is worthwhile or not.

It's OK to know you've achieved so much new business in Q3, but it's not OK to not know how that business was generated.

The more heavily you can segment that data the better. You'll then be in a position to know where you should invest your marketing cash.

Online and offline knowledge is not enough anymore, not since social media and other cool things have come along. Added to this, there can often be a real close correlation between online activity, and associated ad spend, and offline purchases. I saw this daily.

One of the simplest ways of extracting this highly useful information is by simply asking the new customer, both face to face and digitally.

With Falmouth Boat Hire, I came up with a very simple procedure.

Asking the customer.

ASK AT THE POINT OF SALE

It's that simple.

Look at just some of the marketing channels the business used.

- Google adwords
- Strategic partnerships
- Existing business
- Google organic search (SEO)
- Leaflets
- Advertising boards
- Social media
- TripAdvisor
- Van signwriting
- Partner magazines
- Partner guide books (multiple towns)
- Posters
- Various others….

So this is quite some list, and essentially customers could first come across the business in one of those many ways. However, any sales path can be complex.

Here are some examples of how and why tracking purchases is imperative.

- They perform a Google search, then click on a Google Ad, then their doorbell rings and they do not follow through with an online booking – but call us the next day

- They are Facebook users and one of their friends has just "liked" the business Facebook page, so they would begin to look at our pictures and read the stories about the business. They would then go directly to the website and book online or pop down to the quay and book face to face.
- They were hotel guests with one of our partners and they'd seen one of our leaflets, they would then wander down to the quay the following day and book a boat.
- They found us on Google Maps, then see the Falmouth Town Guidebook the next day. The following week they see an advertising board and decide to call us and book online.

I could continue on and on, and all of these are *very real* scenarios. Sales paths are very complex, hard to measure with so many variables.

I know these are very real because I ASKED right at the point of purchase, in fact I didn't just ask, I actually quizzed the customer each and every time. This data was so important that I wrote it into a company procedure document where every member of staff on the quay HAD to quiz the customer, when they were completing the booking process. Questions were along the lines of:

- **FBH**: *"where did you first see us Sir"*
- **Customer:** *"Internet"*
- **FBH:** *"was that a Google search Sir, or an Ad"*
- **Customer:** *I think it was on a tourism website*
- **FBH:** *"do you know which one Sir"*
- **Customer:** (asks wife) *"yes it was XYZ"*

BINGO !!

I now knew I had obtained a referral from XYZ, not the "internet" which is simply far too broad, but I knew the sale was exactly from XYZ.

At the end of the season I would take all of our booking forms and collate the data and make pretty graphs, and this gave us a very accurate picture of how a customer found us in the first instance.

So as you can see this quizzing is important because it tells you if you are spending ad money wisely, and if it is working, or not. Without having a conversation, the customer's response of "Internet" could give you any number of possibilities. Which is fine if you lump things into one pile, like perhaps offline and online marketing, but it's very BAD if the customer finds you first one way but then purchases through a different channel – you could be thinking one of your channels is not working, or working better than it actually is.

QUIZ QUIZ QUIZ...

How can you start?

- Start collecting data. Do you have some already? Do you have a mailing list of customers? Go ahead and create a survey and ask them, get your graphs.
- Create a "point of sale" procedure where your staff must quiz the customer – you are now gathering good data.
- List all of your marketing channels, segment them as much as possible, and put these channels into a list within your ecommerce website, ASK the customer when they purchase.

MAKE FRIENDS WITH THE LOCAL PRESS

I had noticed through local conversation that despite Falmouth Boat Hire being in business for over 50 years in one form or another, there were still so many local people that just were completely unaware of it!

You may be suffering from the same thing. It's easy to think that everyone knows about your business locally, but the chances are they do not at all. Your business is absolutely central to your world and your close friends but you may find you need to raise local awareness too.

Being a tourist destination, and a place where many friends come to visit their seaside friends, I was particularly keen on raising the local awareness levels. I could hear the conversations.. "Hey have you ever been on a boat? You can hire one from down on the quay and go up the river".

I made friends with the local press for this.

Local press is all about publishing content that makes local people buy it. People will buy it for vanity reasons or local gossip. The thing is if you were an editor of a local newspaper of course you would be interested in hearing about news pertaining to local business, therefore feeding your readership with relevancy.

CREATE A PUBLISHER LIST

I created a list of contact names and email addresses for all the local press in Cornwall. This is easily achieved, most of the time the editor's email address can be found on their website.

You then can consider composing a short article about your good news and sending it off to the contact list. I had great success in the local press. Here are just a couple of examples that I wrote and emailed in that may help you formulate your own ideas.

Two Local Businessmen Partner Up and Re-Launch Falmouth Boat Hire

The boat hire business is about to be taken to a new level as Falmouth Boat Hire announces that the business will be operating under a new ownership. Local entrepreneurs Chris Hambly and Chas Cox, who both worked in the business during their younger days are excited to take on the challenge of revolutionizing the business of self-drive boat rentals, particularly in Falmouth. The boat business has been operating from Custom House Quay in one way or another since the 1950s. They've been an integral part of the boating community for literally generations.

Chris Hambly was with Falmouth Boat Hire where he took on an after school job. He went on to become a well-known lecturer in colleges and universities in Cornwall. Chris set up his Internet business in the late 90s, which he later on sold, to establish an Internet consultancy business which he still runs at present.

"I am delighted to have taken on this business with my colleague Chas. It's funny as we both worked as lads on this

business after school back in the 80s, it was our first job and the entrepreneurial bug has never left me", recalls Chris. He adds, "Having run and sold other successful businesses give us the experience to apply the very best process and practice where we can. I'm very much looking forward to taking this business to the next level and continued growth".

Similar to Chris, Chas Cox also took on an after school job at Falmouth Boat Hire. Both he and Chris pursued their interest in boats by joining the Royal Navy. In the 90s, Chas ventured into the financial sector, working in banks. He then proceeded to set up his own independent financial services company.

Chas intends to steer the boat hire industry into a new direction. He shares, "Just like Chris I'm from Falmouth and fell in love with the boat business over 30 years ago. The mechanics of the business have not changed that much in all this time though with our new partnership I'm excited to see it grow to meet the rising demand in Cornwall. We're marketing aggressively and will continue to strive to be the highest quality boat hire operation in Cornwall".

Having spent much of their lives in Falmouth, the boat hire business has become an object of interest to the business partners. They have seen how the business has grown over the years and has challenged them to explore ways to further promote the business. As the partners take on the reins of Falmouth Boat Hire, their aggressive marketing strategies and vision to raise the bar in its operations are set to present the boat hire business as a lucrative endeavour.

About Falmouth Boat Hire Cornwall

The business has a strong industry presence as it provides self-drive boats which can carry up to six passengers. The boats can be rented hourly, half-day, or daily. Customers can set sail and tread the waters of the River Fal. Renting one of the boats will take the passengers to a breath-taking experience of discovering secluded beaches, dining in a cosy restaurant and bar, and taking in the majestic scenery along the River Fal Fishing trips and group picnics can also be enjoyed by families and friends sailing together.

Excellence award for boat firm

Falmouth Boat Hire, the self-drive boats operated business, has received a TripAdvisor Certificate of Excellence.

Joint Directors Chris Hambly and Chas Cox said: "This is such fantastic news for our business, having gained the Certificate of Excellence in 2015 too. We do take our customers' experience very seriously and have invested in our resources and staff to make sure we hit the mark time and time again.

We're blessed to live in such a majestic and beautiful part of the world, we simply must make our customers enjoy their experience to the full. We'd also like to thank our many locals that do take our boats out."

Though a small article this can have very good impact when read by the local residents. If you break down the way I compose it you can see I am reaffirming our commitment to excellence, reinforcing how lucky we are to live here, and thanking the locals too.

You give up things when you hire a self-drive boat from Falmouth Boat Hire. Things like stress, worry and the daily routine.

What makes Falmouth Boat Hire the highest quality boat hire service in Cornwall? There is no magic. It's the amazing place we live in that does it.

When I was a lad I had the best job in the world. During the spring and summer I would leave school and rush down to Custom House Quay to help out on the self-drive boats. It was magical, a young teenage boy working on boats and learning about knots and the tides, getting sun kissed every day, I was hooked.

Becoming a joint Director in Falmouth Boat Hire last year, one of the longest standing boat business in Falmouth, has re-ignited my passion for the sea, for the River Fal, for the majestic sublime place we all live in, Falmouth.

It really does give me a great deal of pleasure seeing customers returning to the Quay having hired a boat for a day, or half a day and seeing how relaxed they are, how comfortable they have become with the outdoors. It's absolutely true that a trip out on one of our boats for the day is literally an amazing experience. Those of you who have been lucky enough to have grown up with boats, will know full well what I refer to here, the experience of calm and tranquillity of the River Fal. Your worries and stress drift away with the salty fresh air, the kids adore it and relish spotting some of the amazing wildlife in the estuary.

It is surely a crime that many local people have not had this opportunity. This is where Falmouth Boat Hire really provides a great service for local people. You can take your family out wildlife spotting, enjoy the river, dine on a picnic and make your way up the estuary in the shadow of Trelissick Gardens, Smugglers Cottage and head towards Malpus, the land that time forgot.

You don't need any experience to hire a boat from us, we give you full instruction and a map, and we are on the end of a phone for your entire trip. It's very much safe family fun, and we can't wait to see your face upon returning, with a beaming relaxed smile and calm kids.

The above article I had published in a local tourism magazine which yielded great results for local bookings. This strategy is simple and effective.

ADVERTISING BOARDS AND MARKETING MESSAGES

I don't rate advertising boards as being that good, though I will say they did prove to be an advertising channel that returned the investment. That really is always the key, a return on investment (ROI). You must know if the money you have spent has returned a profit, otherwise there is simply no point.

e.g. If I spend 200 pounds on artwork, 200 pounds on getting the board made and a further 500 pounds per year on placement I need to be sure that I am not only recouping 900 pounds in that year but I am also making a profit specifically from that investment.

This is why you must measure your advertising as much as possible, it really does make a huge difference. Since I found that not a lot of business came from advertising boards I didn't pursue the activity a great deal. Sure we made our money back, but I found that I could spend that money on other channels and obtain a far higher ROI.

Don't get hung up on having to have advertising boards, if they work then it is awesome for you, but if there are other channels that work better, don't let your ego get in your way, follow the numbers, the money.

When placing the boards we looked for strategic places around the town that could be high visibility locations. We chose places that were a good route into the town for lots of eyeballs. We also placed some very close to the business itself, as signposts for the local footfall, the passing trade.

TIP: You should state the benefits to the customer on the boards, not how good you are.

GUIDE BOOKS

Most towns that have a tourism industry will have some form of local guide book. Someone keen will have seen an opportunity to get as many local businesses invest in advertising and then produce a guide book for the tourists.

Actually you'll find the same kind of books, directories etc. in most trades, these directories or guide books can be useful to bring you business, though again make sure you measure it.

One way I measured the success (or not) of a local guide book was to offer a 10% discount to anyone that booked us through that channel. I set up a coupon code that was only advertised with one advertisement in one guide. Even the web link that people were pointed to was unique. With a unique web link I could tell how many people actually visited our website as a result of seeing our guidebook and with the coupon code I could tell how many people booked.

One such ad was a lovely picture of our boats with a family on board with the following words:

The highest quality boat hire service in Cornwall

Indulge yourself in a self-driven boat trip on the majestic River Fal visiting the quaint Cornish ports and pubs. We guarantee you will come back relaxed and energised. Rent by the hour, full-day or evening. Boats carry six people, no experience necessary, full instruction given, it's safe family fun! 10% discount available here: falmouthboathire.co.uk/guidebook1

Good ad copy with nice stated benefits, an emotional picture is painted. However, after running the ad we found it wasn't making any significant sales. The advertisement was in a guide book with hundreds of other maritime activity advertisements and it quite simply got lost in the crowd. For the price it cost to have the ad in the guide I could make significantly more profit from other channels, channels that are pull, rather than push. That is to say people that are already looking for a service like ours.

TIP: Measure and don't ever be fooled by someone selling it to you as the next best thing, prove it to yourself if it is or not.

CHARITIES

Throughout every year we would receive emails or Facebook messages from people asking for boat rental for giveaways in auctions or raffles.

Firstly, charity is a wonderful thing, I get that, so many good things can be achieved, and we supported many. However, my advice is to make a decision that your business will do x many per year as a policy, and be done with it. You are then in a position to state you would love to help but you have budgeted for x this year.

There is cost involved in giving to charity, a business cost.

Two was enough for us.

Once you have decided on your charities and the events have taken place, you need to maximise the exposure of your goodness by making a song and dance about it in the press, reinforcing your local credibility.

As well as the obvious benefit to the charity cause, these events can indeed help raise awareness for your business too, so choose the best for your business.

The charity formats I tended to favour were the auction style formats where the boat hire experience was auctioned off at an evening event to the highest bidder. These gave exposure to my business amongst all attendees. I usually chose out of town events too, thus trying to spread our reach further to new eyeballs.

TIP: Choose wisely, do not put your business out of a pile of cash just for the love of doing good, you'll fail fast.

YOUR BEST LEADS COME FROM HAPPY CUSTOMERS

Many businesses spend countless amounts of time and financial allocations on marketing, without realising that some of the best promotion can actually be obtained for free. The simple trick to this is good customer service. Customers who are pleased, and even highly impressed by the attention that a company pays to them is worth far more than a company can pay for promotional campaigns. The reasoning behind this comes down to simple psychology, and understanding it will lead to better business practices, as well as stronger leads.

1. WORD OF MOUTH COUNTS

The simple fact is that customers talk. They may converse with friends, acquaintances, and even strangers about recent experiences they have had in the world of service and commerce. Even a passing positive mention of business satisfaction will have an impact, and glowing reviews will really stick in the minds of others. This translates to your business becoming the first consideration when similar products or services are required. I worked hard on raising the work of mouth referrals for Falmouth Boat hire.

2. TRUST ISSUES

When friends and relatives pass on information to one another, there is a certain acceptance of trust that is established in these conversations. When one friend relates a good consumer experience to another friend, the bond that is between the two individuals is transferred over to the business by default. Even if a new customer has yet to use your services, there is already a sense of relationship that has been established through the recommendation. This can lead to an easier time of establishing new connections, and a greater influx of clientele.

3. SATISFACTORY RESULTS EQUALS FREE ADVERTISING

Along with face to face meetings, social media has generated a venue where perfect strangers are willing to relay experiences and endorse businesses as a result of their own interactions. This can be as simple as a blogger recounting their day, and mentioning your business in a good light. This can also extend to satisfied customers making a point of publicly endorsing services either on the company's website under feedback, or in other social media circles. These actions will reach customers that are both distant and near, and will funnel them to your industry. I used social media to help push a few campaigns about our boats around particular events. I also used local hashtags a lot on Twitter, particularly #Falmouth and #Cornwall.

4. THE FRIEND OF A FRIEND PHENOMENON

The friend of a friend phenomenon is somewhat related to building trust, but it is also deeply tied to modern tendencies to always want to be a part of the newest and the best trends. Even if a potential client has heard good things about your business from a more distant source, there is still the association of familiarity and trust, even over degrees of separation. The sense of inclusion is also a factor here, and the more satisfied customers who mention the business name, the greater the chance that the brand can go "viral". Speaking of viral opportunities. I recall when Brad Pitt came to town to film one of his new films. There was an insane buzz in the town about this, and the big time press were all over us to hire boats to swarm the ship the was filming on. The first photograph of "Brad Pitt in Falmouth" was taken from one of my boats, the reporter showed it me on his laptop before he clicked send off to the big daily newspapers in London. Of course I made a huge deal about that on social media.

5. REPEAT BUSINESS AND NEW BUSINESS

Finally, a satisfied customer is also likely to be a repeat customer. The more positive interactions that customers have with your business practices, the more likely they will be to bring friends onto the premises, or to pass along web page information. This is as applicable to a boutique as it is to a café. The enjoyment that is experienced by one person will be passed along, and this can generate interest and hype.

In summary this section looked at knowing where your customers are coming from and the importance of being able to measure it, tied into sales, so understand the sales funnel, the path to purchase is important. Also do work with the local press and consider advertising boards and guide books. Be careful with spending money on charity offerings (it is a business cost) and remember your best leads come from word of mouth.

How can you work smarter?

(Why wouldn't you harness technology and save yourself time?)

Just as we have incorporated labour saving devices into our homes and have applied computer processing power to make everyday tasks simpler, it surely makes sense to incorporate technology into your business, to make you more efficient and save you time. This section will highlight various services available which can not only improve your effectiveness, but also enhance the customer experience.

ONLINE BOOKING SYSTEM

I'm a fan of automation in business, wherever possible. If you can find a task that is manually intensive that can be done by automation and self-service you are saving cash from your bottom line. Not only can you save serious amounts of manual labour with an associated cost you can also enhance the customer experience greatly.

Our target customers were more than used to booking their experiences without speaking to a person. Everyone books flights online, we all secure a hotel room, we rent a car, hell we even order our weekly shopping online. It was the customers that embrace this type of lifestyle I was actively trying to attract.

The way advanced bookings had worked previously was purely over the phone. Either myself, Chas or whichever lad was working on the day would take the call. We'd then have to consult a diary and pen the details in. During the early and late part of each season, we'd not always staff the Quay so calls might come in when we were busy doing many other things so it was certainly disruptive, time intensive and basically flawed.

Added to this labour intensive process we also found that periodically people wouldn't turn up for their booking. Their plans may have changed and because they had not pre-paid they had no real concern, nothing lost. Of course for us a "no show" was expensive, because if we had a booking in our diary we would obviously book the boat out and turn others away, and therefore potentially lose money. And we did! I hated that, I mean it really used to annoy me beyond belief. However, I used this as a learning moment, a challenge to improve. How could I avoid the manual labour of taking the booking, the associated cost of that, and also remove "no shows" for bookings, and the associated costs of that, and streamline the experience for the customer in the process?

An automated online booking system, is how.

It's fair to say that the idea of an online booking system met some resistance from Chas. His initial fears were valid to an extent. Chas couldn't get his head around how it would work on the Quay during the busy season. I had a bit of selling to do here to get his buy-in.

The main issue to overcome was how the lads on the Quay could keep track of online bookings as well as managing the day to day bookings coming in. The main fear was this. What if an online booking came in, when all the boats were already booked manually on the day? How could we be sure payment was made? What would happen with cancellations? All these were valid fears, as the mechanics of how bookings were made was generations old, it was going to be a monumental step change to the business.

BOOKINGBUG

I did a fair amount of research on which booking system to adopt. I even considered building out our own bespoke system, as through my agency, which was now flying again, I had access to good coders. However, it would have been an expensive option and we'd have to go through a lot of pain to get things working as we needed. There is often little point in reinventing the wheel.

Looking at the market I wanted a solution which offered all the features required, at a sensible monthly rental. Things that I needed were:

- Multiple resources (boats)
- Multiple times for resources (the rental periods)
- Multiple calendars (one for each boat)
- Coupon ability (for focused marketing)
- PayPal integration (our payment processing choice)
- SMS ability (had to get text notifications)
- Booking reminders (for us and customers)
- Good customer data capture (I love data, as you know)
- Seamless integration with our website (of course)

After much consideration, and trialling, I decided to use BookingBug, it's really a very good solution that does all of the above very easily.

For the customer the mechanics worked as so:

- Customer views availability of boats online (eventually we only offered our highest profit product online, the half day high for around £97).
- Customer selects time they wish to go (this was sometimes 6 months in advance)
- Customer pays, having agreed to our terms of service.
- Customer receives an email from us with their booking details. Included in this email is a link to our website with car parking details, and some other useful information about suitable clothing etc.
- On the day of the booking the customer would receive an email reminder about their booking.

For the business the mechanics worked as so:

- Customer makes a booking > we got an email and we also got an SMS text message with the booking info.
- In Bookingbug we see the calendar and the booking, and complete customer details, including phone number (very important), and how many people will be on the boat
- Customer email address automatically put into our newsletter system
- Cash automatically into our PayPal account.

So for all of the above we have done nothing, as a business, no labour, no time. I love that.

But it's not just about saving time and labour, it really is ALL ABOUT a better experience for the customer. The customer can self-service when they wish to go, pay up front forming a commitment, get email reminders and signposted to useful information about parking and clothing.

All of this is of course not rocket science is it? This happens in most industries these days, but it was a huge step for Chas and the small self-drive boat business of long standing. I put in a 12 hour time buffer to prevent online bookings for the day itself which prevented double bookings. Online bookings could only be made for the day after and forward of that. Of course we still received phone calls for advance bookings but we briefed the staff to point the customer in the first instance to our website to book online. If the customer resisted of course we'd still take a manual booking and would then add it to our master calendar (in Bookingbug), thus ensuring everything tied in.

BookingBug was around £29 a month, which is peanuts for what it brought to our business. And we could even "freeze" the account in the winter off season, and pay nothing!

Adopting an online booking system where customers could book in advance, pay, receive all the necessary information without us having to do anything saved us hours and hours. It's fair to say this single change was monumental for Falmouth Boat Hire. We started noticing people booking their boat sometimes months in advance, all going on in the background while Chas and I were relaxing and drinking cocktails. Obtaining the money for pre-booked boats months in advance also helped with early season cash flow. You can imagine a seasonal business is tight for cash at the start of each season.

VIRTUAL OFFICE

After a few years of using a van as our office, an office became available on the Quay. When I say office I'm referring to a wooden hut, a shed, positioned on the end of the quay. There were three sheds there and one of the businesses that was using it had moved on due to some family disagreements and started operating from an alternative pier. We jumped at the opportunity to occupy it.

I immediately made some signage for the office in the way of a huge "Self Drive Boats" board position across the top, it was impossible to miss and could be read from the end and top of the quay at the entrance. In addition a few other boards were made that included our best tag lines to draw potential customer interest.

In years gone by touting was the order of the day, though this had since been banned. I understood that decision too, whilst there were apparently several years of complaints, it did make sense. The touting was in fact pretty aggressive and high pressured selling, not a great experience for a tourist taking a walk onto the quay.

The office had electricity and a desk, which was fantastic as we could ensure our phone was always charged and permanently store our buoyancy aids, spare engine and other bits and bobs.

That's all we needed, the basics, we didn't need a board room with 40ft glass tables. It was humble, fit for purpose and cost effective. Don't make the mistake of over stretching your finances on accommodation. Yes, it is important but an eye on the numbers is even more important.

IPAD AND PHONE

In order for our online booking system to work for the business we had to have access to it on the quay, therefore we needed internet connectivity.

We sourced an iPad with a sim contract which meant we could view the booking system and associated details.

The iPad was used to access our booking system, hook up with our PayPal credit card reader for credit card payments, check weather forecasts, tides, email, and occasionally YouTube for fun.

With such agile technology available it also meant we were not restricted to a desktop in the office. In fact taking the iPad and phone home with whoever was on duty was essential. Quite often enquiries and bookings would come in well after 18:00 when we had closed and well before 10:00 when our first lets went to sea. During high season it was not uncommon for the phone to ring before 07:30 while I was still having breakfast. With the iPad within arm's reach I could simply make the booking and ensure all was good for the day. As I said earlier, there is no 9-5 with your own business.

Going forward we basically ran the entire booking side of the business on that iPad, and through cloud based subscription apps. There was no IT support required, no hardware to speak of, if either the phone or iPad broke (it never did) we'd just have asked for it to be replaced.

Of course we had insurance for each item too, and it was worth the additional cost because that boat phone ended up in the water several times, not because of me I must add.

Think about ways that you can use technology like this to mobilise your business, can you access and operate everything you need remotely? Do you really need to visit your business premises to run the back office side?

NEWSLETTERS

Newsletters can be a great way of keeping people in touch with your business. I have used newsletters frequently in many businesses, in fact some newsletters have been THE product itself, for such things as courses or informational products.

For Falmouth Boat Hire a newsletter was not really of much benefit to customers. Although we did have repeat business the majority of business was single-use, that is to say they would enjoy their experience and we'd never see them again, so there was little point in bombarding them with a newsletter, there would just be lots of unsubscribes. However, I did create a newsletter distribution list for two reasons, and with two distinct segments.

1. BUSINESS PARTNERS AND PRESS

This was a distribution list of other local businesses and partners. I could easily keep these partners in the loop (particularly the press) about what we were up to, and if any offers were running that they could talk about with their own clients. You saw those press releases I constructed earlier right? I'd send those things to this segment. If we were offering a special deal for a particular event I would send that out.

2. CUSTOMERS

The other segment was the customers themselves. However, I only sent them a mail twice a year. Once at the start of the season to say we are now open, and one at the end of the season to say we are closed. This was an OK frequency and I was betting on them forwarding it to a friend saying "hey this was amazing, you should check them out too". I also used the opportunity to remind them that we can be found on social media, and if they would be kind enough to write a TripAdvisor review for us. The fact of asking someone to review us on TripAdvisor at the start of the season really helped us get great visibility on the portal. Getting 10 or 11 reviews coming in at similar times seems to trigger TripAdvisor's algorithm into ranking the business well.

The gathering of segment 2 was simple. Bookingbug has an integration section where I could integrate MailChimp with the bookings received. Whenever a customer purchased a hire their email address would be automatically added to this segment. MailChimp is a very intuitive newsletter system, with some fabulous features.

Think about newsletters in your business, particularly if you have repeat business. Capturing a customer's email is really like mining gold whereby you can keep them in the loop and coming back for me. It is far easier to sell to an existing customer than it is to retrieve a completely new one.

A word of caution though, do not leave it too long between email sends, too long and the customer would have forgotten you. You need to time it just right to keep the relationship going. It's well beyond the scope of this book but my online courses expand much further on this.

This section dealt with being smart and agile in your business. We looked at how an online booking system was quite simply revolutionary to the business. We also looked at how we utilised technology to be both mobile and responsive and cost effective. I touched briefly on how a newsletter can be very beneficial for a business.

How much should you charge for your product?

(Not everyone goes with the cheapest quote)

Pricing is the make or break of a business. How far can we push the price yet maintain the perception of value. Conversely how low should a product price become before it just makes too little a profit for the work required. What are the margins, what is the best "ideal" product/price to focus your efforts on. I discuss this in this section.

PRICING ANALYSIS

When I first started back on the Quay, Chas was selling hour long boat hires for just £25, and half day hires (4 hours) for £65. The type of customer that this attracted was not the type of customer for our business. We'd get the type of person that wants everything for nothing - the moon on a stick!

When you price things so low, you can expect to get customers that live in the world of bargains. Added to this, we'd get people asking things like if they could have 30 minutes, and pay even less. This type of crowd are the fairground crowd, people looking for a couple of laps around the harbour whilst eating an ice cream, *"come in number 4 your time is up"*. We were not a fairground attraction; we had potential to be better, much better.

As well as the wrong type of customer being attracted I wondered how Chas made any money at all. I did the math on boats available, cost per hour, hours in a day and soon worked out far greater potential on many levels.

The pricing had to change, and of course I had to manage Chas and help him see the business could do more. Time to bring on our A game.

PRICING SERVICES

Pricing a service can be a tricky thing, particularly when competition exists. First you need to look at the potential you have for value perception and if you have the corresponding service to match with the value. Next you need to figure out the ideal customer, and finally you should consider your competitors.

We knew the experience we were offering was awesome if we could improve both the quality and condition of the boats and customer service. We also knew by now what our ideal customer was - you remember how we did that analysis? That just left us looking at our competition.

THE COMPETITORS

We had three main competitors operating from the same river. Whilst not operating from the same physical space, they were on the same river and available somewhere in Google searches.

The competitors had a few disadvantages.

1. Their boats were smaller, and did not have a closed cabin (not ideal if it rains)
2. Their boats could only take 5 people (We were the only business with a licence to take 6)
3. Their online marketing coverage and footprint was nowhere close to ours

Given these disadvantages it didn't take me long to come to the conclusion we were the highest quality boat hire service in Cornwall. You'll recall I wrote that into our strategic objective. Therefore, it was important to differentiate from the competition, make this difference in quality really obvious and shout loudly about it in our marketing material, and I did.

It was important to price certain customers out of the market completely and instead attract those customers with disposable income, therefore changing the sale to our ideal target customer.

We moved swiftly from 25/hr to 30/hr to 35/hr and then settled finally on 40/hr.

I must admit I have read before that one great way of turning around a business is to raise the prices immediately by one 1/3rd, I raised by 2/3rd. Now a 60% hike in fees may sound like a lot, but I can tell you the business probably could have taken a further hike. Because most of our customers were new business, they'd never been presented with the cheap option.

So we became more expensive than all the competitors immediately.

Am I crazy? No, it works.

We were the "highest quality boat hire company in Cornwall" and we had prices to match that statement too.

You have to bring in psychology here with regards to price framing and marketing. If you get into a price war with competitors and try to beat them on price it is a fast road to the end, the death of your business. You have to sell on benefits and advantages for the customer, the lifestyle, and that's exactly what we did.

We started noticing a much higher grade of customer renting our boats, more families, more conscientious, and frankly far less hassle. Our boats went aground less, were almost never late back in, almost no complaints, and compliments on what great value it was and that they'd have paid more!

Don't get hung up on your competitors prices, it is far more important to see how your products/service differentiate. Once you have found a differentiation can you amplify it? Can you find something in your service that your competitors cannot compete with, that's the value you can add. This leads me onto framing.

FRAMING SERVICES

Framing is simply having different services/products and associated different prices. Some low, some high some in the middle.

Our low rate was £40/hr, and then each successive hour on top was another £20.

1hr = 40

2hr = 60

3hr = 80

4hr = 95

We deducted the £5 off the 4 hours as the 4 hour let for us was the golden sale. We could get one boat working a half day in the morning, turn it around and send it back out for another half day in the afternoon. So one single boat could earn us close to £200 in a day on half day.

A single boat on single 1hr rental could earn us £320 a day (8hrs x £40/hr). However, we pushed hard for half days as getting 8 x 1hr lets for every single one of our boats would be highly intensive work and a LOT of customers to attract and to process.

Getting single 1hr bookings was disruptive to our half day hires, as it meant we would potentially be losing out on a half day for £95. Sure we'd get £40/hr but it would have to be booked out twice to get £80, and then burn more petrol, take more manpower and customer service. The half day was simply the easiest least maintenance option and also the absolute best experience for the customer, and do not underestimate that importance.

We were delighted to see our TripAdvisor reviews come in, all pertaining to the half day hires, which if you remember was the only option we offered to be booked online. It was long enough to explore all of the river, but not long enough for customers to get bored, which is what the full day hire used to create, and therefore why we withdrew it. Customers on the half day hire would come back in wanting just a tiny bit more, a bit like the last song of the band before you scream for the encore.

You see, it really is about tapping into your ideal customer. I'd liked to have operated an exclusive boat hire service charging 1000s of pounds a day per boat, but for that it would need different boats and a very different strategy.

The point is that there is an ideal market and customer for each business, operating at each end of the spectrum from pennies to millions of pounds. The secret is matching the branding, service, marketing, experience and price together, aligning it, framing it, and framing the products within in.

I don't know about you but I prefer doing less work for more money and if you can frame your services correctly you can obtain the most bang for buck.

Frame the lifestyle, make it work for you. Happy customers will make your business happy, and you happy as a consequence.

CREDIT CARDS

As we started changing pricing and framing our products to attract clients with disposable income it became very apparent that we had far more people asking if they could pay by credit card. I started considering how we could take credit card payments.

Prior to my introducing credit card transactions into the business in 2013, the customer had to always pay with cash. Not offering the possibility to pay by card was simply, in my mind, really bad customer service.

The scenario would be that a customer would come to the end of the quay, probably a long way from their parked car and want to book a boat only to be told "sorry sir we only take cash". I'd have hated to be on the receiving end of that and would have been dismayed that a business in this day and age would not take a credit card, it just stinks of unprofessionalism, it's really bad customer service, period.

So if this is you, fix it immediately. Offer cards.

The solution was really straightforward, we just obtained a card reader machine from PayPal, that links up through Bluetooth to an iPad connected to the Internet. Punch in the total, offer it to the customer for their pin, and we then get the funds immediately into our PayPal account, it was so easy Chas couldn't believe it.

The added bonus of going down this route was although there was a small transaction processing fee, there was no recurring rental or fees on the card reader, something that comes with lots of credit card payment packages. The processing fee was around 1.5% which is nothing to us really on a £100 transaction.

The benefits for experience for the customer was fabulous, professional and slick. Upon payment confirmation the system would also ask if the customer would like an email receipt. Perfect, no need for us to have a printer in our shed, no ongoing costs, all electronic.

There are several solutions around that do this, not just PayPal, but seeing as PayPal have been in this business longer than most they have it down very well.

Don't penny pinch either.   If the service makes the customer's experience awesome, it's usually a good move.

CUSTOMER DISCOUNTS

Too much customer discount will damage any business. 'Mate's rates' will kill a business. I made a decision that we simply did not offer any discount whatsoever. You just have to stick to your guns, and tell the customer "sorry it is our policy, we do not offer discounts".

At the start of the season, and the end of the season we would come across what I call the cheapskates.

The questions would be like this:

"it's not so busy now can you offer us some discount for this time of year?"

Or

"We just want the boat for 30 mins, can we do that for a cheaper price?"

It's was a no from us every time - never under value your products, ever. If the customer doesn't want to pay the price, do not be desperate, be polite and refuse. If like me you are trying to create a reputation for being the best, the highest quality, there is a perception of value that comes with it.

This might sound harsh but this is a business you are running, not a charity.

In summary this section considered the pricing model for your business and I ask you to consider what is the best product for your business, what makes the best margin. Look at how you add value, what differentiates you from your competitors? Amplify this difference and strive for creating the perception of value and bring out the benefits for customers. Also if you are not processing credit cards do it, I mean really?

How will you build your network?

(How to make friends and influence people)

Business has always been about relationships, both with your customers and suppliers. And the smart businesses also go out of their way to build strong relationships with their peers and even competitors. Having a strong network can bring you new business, strengthen existing contracts, and keep you in the information loop. This section will introduce you to the process of networking and forming partnerships, giving you tips on how to choose what's best for your business.

NETWORKING

Your business may well be selling to consumers just as ours was. This is known as a Business to Consumer (B2C) situation. However, if you begin to think about the business community which you are situated within you may find some interesting opportunities. If you're not already networking with your local business community, it may be time to start to yield lots of great ideas and potential partnership and referrals.

Regardless of where you are located there will typically be some business groups that get together periodically to network.

CHOOSE WISELY

When you track these groups down my advice is that you do not go to every single networking event going. You'd just be spreading yourself far too thinly and you'll never get to know anyone particularly well; you'll always be just partially known.

Also stay away from the ones that charge a fee for introductions and annual subscriptions or dodgy enforced referring. Those are way too closed and like an old gentlemen's club, old boys school, masonic style, useless. Look for progressive and dynamic, but not too shiny and gimmicky, you need to seek out authenticity.

What I found important for networking was to get to know a handful of local business people really well. I used to attend one such networking event every Thursday morning for breakfast.

The "Business Breakfast" or Falmouth Business Club is an event hosted by a local guy called Andy Coote.

Each week around 15 to sometimes as many as 50 people would attend a local hotel for breakfast. There would be a theme each week around a business topic and good discussion would come from it.

I remember walking into this "Business Breakfast" meet for the first time right after I lost that huge consultancy client, you know when I hit rock bottom. I walked in penniless wearing my handmade Saville Row suit that I had gotten tailored a few years previously. I was full of fear and anxiety, but knew I had to build again and start knocking on doors and opening conversations, get known, be available, and make friends.

I almost walked out the door when I soon discovered we had to all individually introduce ourselves, and give an elevator pitch about what we do, to the whole group! It felt like what I imagine therapy or counselling must be like, I was feeling way outside of my comfort zone.

However, when I began my introduction I immediately found people were interested in listening to what I had to say about digital marketing, along with growing and selling a business, and my experience, the room seemed captivated. I didn't tell them my world had just fallen apart.

That social group really played a part in helping to get my mojo back.

IT'S ABOUT MAKING BUSINESS FRIENDS

These networking events should never be considered as the place you expect to generate sales from immediately. You can't walk in unknown, push out your elevator pitch and expect sales. Business to business doesn't work that way.

You should look at these events as a way to build trust and credibility that cultivates long term relationships that generate referrals way down the pipeline. Andy's networking club worked very well for me. As well as boat hire referrals I also got a lot of digital marketing contract work for local businesses too. Before too long I was "the guy" in that club for all things digital. I was building websites, consulting, gaining referrals and impressive LinkedIn testimonials. The boats were also getting known and additional business came from that too.

DON'T PUT IT ABOUT EVERYWHERE

In summary, don't jump at every single networking opportunity, you'll get to know nobody very well. I've known networking socialites that seem to visit everything and everywhere as often as possible like dogs sniffing out new scent. I've seen the same people years down the road without a business.

It's easy to get wrapped up in the idea of being in business, yet taking your eye off the ball and not actually building it, growing it. Don't be flitting here there and everywhere. Choose one networking group you can commit to and build relationships, be helpful, add value to the group. It will pay you back further down the road.

For me these are almost like therapy, and I relay to you that it's important to talk through your pain with other people that are probably going through exactly the same issues as you are in their own business. Fears, loss of contracts, staff issues, low cash flow, accountancy, tax bills, awkward customers etc.

STRATEGIC PARTNERSHIPS

What are strategic partnerships?

The chances are that around your territory there will be lots of other businesses selling things quite different to yours, perhaps even in completely different markets.

You might be a website designer, and there may be a vehicle signwriting business near you. Now what if all of the customers walking into the signwriting business could also know about your business?

Again, think for a moment. A lot of the people going into a signwriting business are likely running a business and therefore interested in advertising, perhaps they are starting their new business, they'd need a website.

Perhaps your business bakes cupcakes. What other businesses around you would be frequented by your target customers? Probably not a plumber's merchant, or a steel fabrication firm. I would imagine an event organisation business would, or a wedding planner.

Do you have a fitness centre? What large business is around that could offer all of their employees discounted monthly memberships to your fitness gym?

HOTELS

For Falmouth Boat Hire I made key strategic partnerships with the two biggest hotels in the area. Hotels have tourists, tourists want to do things. Most hotels have shelves full of leaflets with activities to do, which is a noisy place for your business to stand out and to be seen amongst all those other shitty leaflets.

I bypassed those leaflet jungles by making a strategic partnership where the hotel would put our offer on their website (good for SEO), and also make guests aware upon check-in. In return I gave the two hotels exclusivity and agreed not to make the offer to other hotels that were their competitors.

I recall creating one specific partnership through a girl called Lena. Lena was a tall bubbly blonde woman with a dimpled warm smile that had recently landed the job of Business Development Manager in one of the hotels I wanted a presence with. In business to business (B2B) situations it's always about the people, the relationships, which is somewhat different from a business to consumer (B2C) type of business. People will buy and make decisions with people they like personally, and have rapport with. They need to trust you, they need to like what you say and how you are. I had a head start with Lena, I knew her father from years ago from when I used to crew in local yacht racing. So Lena and I through her dad had common ground upon which to begin our business relationship. I also knew that being new Lena was really looking for some good quick wins.

I chose two hotels, to play them off against each other a little bit, you can't let them think they are in too a strong a position. Competition is good.

In addition I made a few smaller partnerships with accommodation providers, like holiday lets, enabling them to sell boat hire holiday packages! Happy days for us, we're now getting partners selling for us.

FOOD SUPPLIERS

Falmouth had a new delicatessen in town that was roaring ahead with trade and exposure. A very well branded business with well thought out local produce on offer and good design as well as fitting in perfectly with our ideal customer's interests and values. This place was just up the street from us so I popped along for a chat about some ideas that would work for the both of us.

I pitched it to the Manager, that we could offer a new product ourselves which would be called a "Cornish River Experience". This Cornish River Experience would be a boat rented for a day with a readymade high quality Cornish picnic in an impressive hamper basket. The benefit for the delicatessen was of course they would make money from us purchasing the picnic, plus of course being able to use the story in their marketing messages.

The product worked out very well. We offered the product for sale through our booking system which proved very popular with couples. You can imagine how romantic this experience was. Couples turn up on a beautiful summer day, collect their boat and enjoy a wonderful Cornish produce food hamper in a delightful wicker basket.

All we had to do was notify the deli when we had an order in (all paid for up front online) and they would bring the picnic down to us on the quay on the day. Fantastic. We made a small margin on the picnic itself but we made a good profit on the boat hire, and it gave us a good high priced exclusive product, which also helped us frame the pricing of our other services.

You need to look at these partnerships as deals, what can you get from them? And in return what can you offer? A hotel offering exclusive boat hire discount is another tool the hotel can use to help sell their packages.

TIP: Think creatively on potential partnerships, you will find many opportunities around you. The opportunities should cost you nothing, perhaps just a small discount off your price in return for lots of additional sales, you build that discount into your marketing budget.

In summary we talked about the importance of networking, not only for referrals but damn fine support and to give you a sense of you're doing ok. I then asked you to think about strategic partnerships as being an excellent way of generating further business. Think non competing services also selling into your niche market.

How will you know when to sell your business?

(It's the final piece of the jigsaw, but does it fit right?)

So you've worked hard for years to build your business, taking it from humble beginnings to become an efficient, networked, profitable enterprise. You may want to run it forever, but you may also want to realise the fruits of your labour, cash in on all your hard work, and maybe even go on to a new challenge. This section will explain how to value your business and find the right buyer.

SELLING THE BUSINESS

So we've reached the main point of what we were working towards with Falmouth Boat Hire - the sale!

A lot took place during those 5 years when I restarted with the boats.

We had gone from a somewhat ragged, unbranded, cash only, inexpensive boat hire offering, attracting the wrong customers, and working with outdated processes, to a professional customer-centric business, with consistent branding attracting families with disposable income.

All the way on this journey we had kept referring to the Strategic Objective, the guidelines, the mission, the point, our plan. Sure, we had made some adaptations on the way, some tweaks, but the main spine of the Strategic Objective was running consistently through the entire business.

At every opportunity we put a process in place, a repeatable way of doing a task. If a task is repeatable it can be documented and anyone can learn to do it. Also if the process is documented it can be measured against the description, and changed if a better way can be found.

The whole point of course was to create what is known as a turn-key business. That is to say, a business that is ready to go, complete, nothing to do but hand over the keys to a new owner that can unlock on their first day and be up and running.

We'd achieved it, the final parts of the puzzle were in place and we genuinely felt we had taken the business as far as we possibly could without a serious amount of investment to take it to a completely new level.

That new level may well have been acquiring other related businesses to increase our turnover and assets, our reach, and our footprint. We could have had conversations with other local businesses that would have been a suitable fit. However, we felt we were done, we were ready to divorce ourselves and move on. Chas was wanting to slow down a little and I was more interested in business that is less labour intensive, like writing books, and designing digital courses.

So in order to start selling the business we began to have a few conversations with some brokers who duly valued our business. The valuations that came back were similar to what we had in mind.

Neither of us were experts in business valuation, we didn't know really where to start though we had a rough idea of what we thought it might be worth. I had a conversation with a friend who specialises in business acquisitions though. His general rule of thumb is that a business' value is six times the yearly profit.

Another way to value is to consider the value of the fixed assets and then consider the value of the earning potential of the goodwill of the business. Naturally all businesses have very different structures, you'll need to seek advice here. If you go to a broker they will simply look at the numbers, the accounts, and make a calculation. I will say that in my experience the buyer will pay what they think it is worth, particularly for a lifestyle business like ours.

For Falmouth Boat Hire we always knew we were selling a lifestyle business. That is to say, someone that wanted to work outside for six months of the year, deep in Cornwall. We thought that a perfect buyer would be perhaps someone that may have been in the armed forces and retired mid 40s with a military pension, a lump sum of cash that wanted to move to a beautiful part of the world and play with boats.

David Blumenstein a native New Yorker business consultant friend of mine said that the first thing we should do when ready to sell is to go to the competition first to see if they would be interested.

You'll not believe what happened next!

Completely out of the blue a guy called Steve (who ran another boat hire business in Cornwall) called us and asked if we had considered selling Falmouth Boat Hire. This was not at all related to conversations with brokers or agents, it was just incredible serendipity.

Chas took the initial phone call from Steve, he then explained to me that Steve was interested. At this point you can well imagine how excited I was, I think on the phone I even said "fuck off Chas", out of surprise and assumed it was another of his crappy gags, the type we always wind each other up with, often brutally. But this was real.

It's a strange feeling indeed when someone calls you up and says "hey I want to buy your business". I've had this twice now, and I must say I do love that feeling. It's somewhat hard to describe it, it's like you want to fist bump the air, do a little silly dance shouting "yes yes yes" or some crazy moon walk through the kitchen spurting "who's the man, who's the man". It's a feeling that completely validates your efforts, and your hard work. You know those times when you seem to be working harder than anyone else, while they're relaxing, you are grafting away? That effort you put in is for these moments, you're there - someone sees value in what you've created and wants it enough to hand over dollops of cash for it.

I believe Steve calling us was also not totally random. Steve had done his research. It turns out he had even hired a boat the season before and had experienced what we were about. He must have been impressed with what he saw, the professionalism, the slickness, the attention to detail, in essence the result of our Strategic Objective in creating a very well-oiled turnkey machine, turn up for work and make money.

TIP: Don't settle for the quotes from brokers, these are almost always based solely on the numbers. You can think about lifestyle, you can think about what someone might have to borrow, and what those fees would be, are they achievable for the price of sale?

THE BUYER

Was he a good fit?

This may sound like a strange question. Why would we care if Steve was a good fit for the business? Why not simply take the money and run?

Well, you can probably tell this was more than just a business for us. We had a lot of history with the quay, the boats, and the entire community surrounding the quay. We had given significant periods of our life to Falmouth Boat Hire, it had been our lifestyle for a long while.

The sale would always be a love hate/type of affair. Sure, Chas and I were delighted we'd reached the goal, but we also experienced feelings of apprehension, or were perhaps a little perturbed that the lifestyle would no longer be there. I think Chas probably experienced these feelings more deeply than me to be honest, and understandably so. Chas had been with the boats as an adult for about 20 years! We both really did love the lifestyle, but alas all things must come to an end and this was absolutely the correct time to sell from a business point of view.

So of course we wanted the best for the future of the business. The worst thing that could have happened is that someone bought the business and then had no clue how to operate it, and it failed. This would not have been good on many levels. If the business failed with the new owner, we'd have not created a turnkey business and the legacy would be terrible. We'd both have felt responsible and the history of the business would have ended. That is not something we'd have ever wanted, and I'd never have been able to write this book!

Steve was a perfect buyer. Remember I mentioned previously that my consultant friend David suggested we should approach the local competition first? Well, Steve operates a boat hire business about an hour away from Falmouth. Though not direct competition with Falmouth itself, he was certainly competition for Cornwall as a whole, and we certainly targeted Cornwall as a whole with our advertising, specifically through both Google Ads and search engine optimisation. I'm 100% sure we would have taken business from Steve over the years when customers made a search for something like "boat hire in Cornwall".

As the "Boat Phone" was with Chas the evening Steve called, Chas became the contact guy for the entire process, pretty much. I must take my hat off here to Chas for he is an excellent people person. There couldn't have been a better person for Steve to communicate with through the sale.

We arranged a meet with Steve in the Chain Locker pub. The Chain Locker sits on the corner of the quay, the watering hole of many salty seafaring types down the centuries. I believe the pub was one of the first in Falmouth. It must be around 500 years old, with its low ceilings, crooked walls and rabbit warren connecting corridors the Chain Locker has many secrets and stories of times gone by. You can only imagine how much business and deals have been made over a handshake in the Chain Locker, and we were about to make another.

TIP: Make sure your buyer is the right choice for your circumstance. It's important to see the close out and the resultant fallout (if any) is in your interest.

NEGOTIATIONS

The first meeting was a little guarded, more than cautious you might say, certainly from Chas and myself. You never know if these things are genuine or if someone is trying to get the recipe for your secret sauce. We had to be sure Steve was legitimate and wasn't here just to find out about all the cool stuff we did, that he could use himself.

First impressions count I think and Steve came across as a real boatman, sun kissed face with deep lines and happy smile it was clear he spent a lot of time outside.

As we warmed to each other we began to talk more openly about our business and how we operated. We started drawing comparisons on how each of the businesses operated, and also highlighted where the big differences were, which were numerous to be honest.

Steve's boat business was very much "old school", which I'm sure he'd admit to. Stick a sign up and wait for passing trade, something which I had long ceased to focus on for Falmouth Boat Hire, whilst still a good revenue stream it was certainly not the main one any longer. The biggest differences between Steve's approach to his business and ours was in the marketing, branding, and unsurprisingly the online component, which showed a monumental difference.

In summary it is important you feel good about the sale, the person buying and if they are a good fit. You will find a variety of reasons to consider for your own personal circumstance. As a seller you are not obliged to produce anything particularly legal as that is always the buyer's responsibility. They may ask for an inventory list and of course detailed accountancy figures are expected, this is normal. However, I personally wouldn't hand over any assets (including documents such as your Strategic Objective) until the cash was in my bank, it's your business manual, the secret sauce. If a contract is produced by their legal team definitely get your legal contact to check on your behalf, sometimes those things can be quite big and full of legal jargon and you don't want to get yourself tied up contractually in anything that doesn't work for you.

Summary

As I sit here now, writing this section of the book, on a plane to Frankfurt, I feel I must emphasise again what a game changer the online aspect brought to the value of the business.

You've probably understood that for your own business bringing in online technology, be it credit card transactions, booking systems, search optimisation, newsletters, social media etc can also have a major impact on the visibility and associated profit of your business.

However, it is easy to be fooled, or hoodwinked into solutions offered by many a local hustler. I appreciate it is hard to understand many of these methods if you are not used to them or you have been unsuccessful with them previously.

My advice is to always look at how the technology will benefit the customer that should be your single most important consideration. Secondly, can it bring automation to the business, can it lower overheads and can it increase profit.

Now I have finished this short book I have also launched a full blown suite of online courses about these themes on my Academy web site chrishambly.com

You can follow links and sign up for a fully-fledged online course all about these topics where I expand each section and include videos, pdf downloads and study guides. If you're looking for help and support in your own efforts do pop along and sign up for that, I'll see you there.

It's been fun writing this book and if you have enjoyed it please do give it a review, it's my first "book" and hopefully not my last, I've enjoyed the experience of writing it for you.

I wish you the very best in your business endeavours. Keep believing.